QUARTER HORSES
A Story of Two Centuries

QUARTER HORSES

A Story of Two Centuries

Robert Moorman Denhardt

Foreword by Richard Chamberlain

UNIVERSITY OF OKLAHOMA PRESS
NORMAN AND LONDON

To Jack F. Hutchins

Without the assistance of Mr. Jack and Miss Louise
a most significant chapter in my life could not
have been so successful—including whatever part I
had in re-establishing the Quarter Horse.

LIBRARY OF CONGRESS CATALOG CARD NUMBER: 67–15580

ISBN: 0–8061–2285–4

8   9   10   11   12   13   14   15   16   17   18   19   20   21   22

CONTENTS

ILLUSTRATIONS

FOREWORD

by Richard Chamberlain

BOB DENHARDT WAS my friend. I'm proud to say that. By the
time I met the man (I was in my twenties and he was seventy),
Denhardt had already had a strong influence on me and my life, as
he had on the lives of everyone who had ever thrown a leg across a
Quarter Horse, who had ever watched a Quarter Horse in competition or at work, or who had merely admired the breed from afar. In
the late 1930s, Bob Denhardt distinguished himself as the quintes-
sential historian and chronicler of the Quarter Horse. Today, he is
widely recognized as the person who pulled together the disparate
interests, personalities, and horses that became the American Quarter
Horse Association.

I love Quarter Horses, and so do a lot of other people. In the
Colonial America of the late 1600s and early 1700s, "sportsmen"
and "gentlemen" were crossing the so-called Chickashaw ponies of
Spanish origin with blooded English stallions to produce what became known as the "Celebrated Colonial Quarter-of-a-Mile Running Horse," a match-race horse that could run two furlongs (440
yards, or a quarter mile, usually right up the village main) in some
twenty-five or twenty-six seconds, a fabulous speed at the time.
Bred initially for its running ability, and later for its durable de-
pendability, even temperament, and innate cow sense, the Quarter
Horse—or Steel Dust, or Billy, or Cold Deck, or whatever it was
called in a given locale—became the horse that settled the West.

As much as people cared for the Quarter Horse, however, they
showed little interest in keeping records. No registry or stud book
was kept, and most horsemen did not know the pedigree of their
own horses for more than a generation or two back. Some of the

better breeders knew their own sires' top line, but even they were generally unaware that similar blood was being used by other breeders in different areas of the country.

Bob Denhardt changed all that. Denhardt was born on Flag Day, June 14, 1912, the son of an Episcopalian minister in the Northern California town of Colusa. His family did not have horses, but even as a little boy, he was fascinated by the creatures. Bob told me that one of his earliest memories was of the time he caused a runaway by throwing a rock at a horse pulling a Chinese vegetable vendor's wagon.

As Denhardt grew up, he became a bit more responsible, but age never dimmed his interest in horses and things Western. As a teenager, he rode in the Red Bluff rodeo, and he whiled away his summer days helping a friend break horses in the hills east of town. Denhardt survived the horses, high school, and rodeo, and graduated in 1930. While that was not a particularly good year for facing the world as a new high-school graduate, it was, on the other hand, probably no worse than the following year, when he faced the world as a new college flunk-out. Denhardt then put in a year or so working for a state senator, and spent most of his free time riding a little mare that he could almost call his own. She made a big impression on him, and Denhardt, a bit more mature and a little more willing to study, returned to get his sheepskin from the University of California at Berkeley.

While at Berkeley, he researched the introduction of Spanish horses and their spread in the New World, a project that was supposed to be his Ph.D. dissertation but instead became his first book, *The Horse of the Americas,* published by the University of Oklahoma Press. In the meantime, Denhardt took a position teaching history at the Agricultural and Mechanical College of Texas (now Texas A&M University). In Texas, he became interested in the Steel Dust horses that predominated the better ranches. That interest led him to research the bloodlines that had created the fastest, most versatile breed of horse that the world had ever seen.

The rest, as they say, is history, much of it recounted in this book. *Quarter Horses: A Story of Two Centuries* is the definitive work on the origins and development of the breed. The book is far more than a mere discussion of the Quarter Horse itself. Most people today tend to think of the Quarter Horse as a Western horse, a ranch or rodeo horse—the cowboy's horse. Others also acknowledge its more esoteric uses as a racehorse, a polo mount, an animal suited to the hunt field, and even Grand Prix jumping. And indeed, beyond question, representatives of the breed excel in all those capacities and more, to the point that people unfamiliar with the Quarter Horse often doubt the claims. Of what the horse is capable should come as no surprise; the Quarter Horse was bred from the combined bloods of already-established breeds of horses, and the real surprise would have been if it were less capable, less versatile. One can neither understand nor fully appreciate the breed without a concomitant understanding and appreciation of its roots, and one cannot claim to have fully researched those roots without having carefully studied *Quarter Horses: A Story of Two Centuries.*

Bob Denhardt lived a life rich and full, a life in which he took much inspiration from a young lady named Sarah Brim, whom he met on a blind date. Married after going out together half a dozen times, she made him a father and, later, a grandfather in the half century they spent together before he died of cancer in the spring of 1989. The first executive secretary of the American Quarter Horse Association, the ramrod of a major Quarter Horse breeding operation in Texas, the editor of *The Western Horseman* in Colorado Springs, the author of books and articles too numerous to list, an international traveler, and one of the first two people inducted into the Quarter Horse Hall of Fame, Denhardt was a man who, perhaps most important of all, knew himself.

Beyond that, however, he showed me, a fellow horse addict, that it is possible to make a living observing and reading and writing about the greatest breed of horse on the face of the earth. For that, I am eternally grateful.

Bob Denhardt was my friend.

PREFACE

ONE COULD ARGUE that any author is an egotist. After all, he expects people to read what he writes. A would-be historian has an advantage, since he may feel that what he writes will add to human knowledge. Books have been written for many reasons, not the least of which is to please the public. Cunninghame Graham in *The Ipané* says that books are written for vanity, hope of gain, and even, sometimes, to please the writer. So be it.

This particular book has, in addition, another excuse. There are no other books covering the history of the Quarter Horse. All that is available is an article here and a chapter there. If you know the past, you can understand today and anticipate tomorrow. For this reason the serious Quarter Horse breeder and enthusiast cannot use his horses wisely today or mate them intelligently for tomorrow without knowledge of his breed's origin, development, and principal bloodlines. The background of this great American breed is not only information of vital interest to the consummate horseman, but also a fascinating story in its own right.

I have been fortunate in having known most of the important early breeders and in having seen many of the greatest sires. It soon became apparent, as I was collecting information on the breed, that it was impossible to be sure that all details were correct. The accounts of eyewitnesses varied, not only among themselves, but with the scarce contemporary records. The main current of the story was not, however, changed by this conflict. One can argue about Peter McCue's pedigree but not about his existence or his influence on the Quarter Horse.

The footnotes should not cause the reader any qualms. They are meant to be like a blaze along a forest trail, leading the curious reader deeper into the woods of his choice.

In traveling across the western states for thirty years, *poco más o menos*, taking notes and talking horses, I have been helped by hundreds of different people interested in horses. To list them all for the credit they are due would be impossible, to leave some out would be unfair—so to all who contributed, *muchas gracias*.

A portion of the material incorporated in this book has appeared in somewhat different form in other books and magazines, such as *The Quarter Horse, The Cattleman, The Western Livestock Journal, The Western Horseman*, and *The Quarter Horse Journal*. As the years roll by, it is easy to forget where one lays things down.

Colusa County, California   ROBERT M. DENHARDT

QUARTER HORSES
A Story of Two Centuries

1. COLONIAL BEGINNINGS

Ω Ω Ω Ω EUROPEAN BACKGROUND

THE AMERICAN QUARTER HORSE had his beginnings with the appearance of the first horse. However, his history as an individual type did not start until the horse was brought to America from Europe. One could generalize and say that the dams of these first Quarter Horses were of Spanish origin, as we know that Spanish horses were running wild in the backwoods of the southern English colonies when they were established. It is also true that the sires were, for the most part, imported from England, like that greatest of early Quarter Horse progenitors, Janus. Let us trace the sires to England, and the dams to Spain, so that we will know something of the stock that produced the American Quarter Horse.

The earliest English importations were probably Hobbies and Galloways, brought over by the Cavaliers who settled on the southern Atlantic seacoast after the death of Charles I in 1649. Good Celtic blood of similar type was, in the next hundred years, to fashion the Thoroughbred. The Thoroughbred horse was not considered an established breed until 1728 when the Godolphin Arabian, which was probably a Barb, was brought into England.

The sturdy little Galloways—note how their description fits that of the Colonial Quarter Horse—lived in the district of Galloway on the shores of the Solway Firth in the south of Scotland. According to Youatt,[1] tradition had the breed starting from a few horses that escaped when the Spanish Armada was driven against the shores and wrecked in 1588. The horses were said to have been

---

1 Considerable information relative to the origin and development of the Thoroughbred horse can be found in *The Horse*, by William Youatt. Even better in some respects is the book *Origin and Influence of the Thoroughbred Horse*, by William Ridgeway.

around 14 hands high, bright bay or brown, with black legs, small heads, and peculiarly clean legs. A contemporary of Herbert[2] described them as being 14½ hands high, elegant in shape, and gentle of disposition. One was twice ridden 150 miles at a stretch without stopping except to eat, arriving at its destination with as much ease and spirit as when it departed. Another Galloway, belonging to a Mr. Sinclair of Kirby Lonsdale, at Carlisle, performed the extraordinary feat of traveling one thousand miles in one thousand hours. Herbert continues by saying that the Narraganset horse of America and the Galloway of England "were nearly, if not altogether identical, both in characteristics and descent."[3] There seems little reason to doubt that the breed was brought to America by the early settlers.

One of the most important strains to influence the Colonial Quarter Horse was the pony developed by the Cherokee and Chickasaw Indians.[4] The Chickasaws had, of course, obtained their horses from the Guale settlements of Spain and the Cherokees from the Southwest as well as from the Southeast. Even that early,

[2] Henry William Herbert, *Frank Forester's Horse and Horsemanship of the United States*, II, 31. For information on Henry Herbert see note 16 below.

[3] *Ibid.*, 33.

[4] The relationship between the Cherokees, the Chickasaws, and the Quarter Horse is as interesting as it is nebulous. The following references are pertinent. Paul Albert was one of the first to point out the importance of these Indian horses in the development of the modern western horse in "Romance of the Western Stock Horse," *Western Horseman*, April, 1936. Perhaps the earliest reference is found in Adam Gordon's, *Travels in the American Colonies*, 384. He wrote in 1764. Another reference which points out the excellence of these horses is J. F. D. Smyth, *A Tour in the United States of America, etc.*, I, 361–64, written in 1781. Edward Eggleston, in the January, 1884, issue of *Century Magazine*, commented on the horses. Still another valuable article is Sol Torey's "Quarter Horse and Chickasaw," *Western Horseman*, July, 1942; also, H. D. Smiley's "The Cherokee Side of the Quarter Horse," *The Quarter Horse Journal*, December, 1954. See also Nelson C. Nye *The Complete Book of the Quarter Horse*, 23. He quotes Dr. John B. Irving ("The Turf in South Carolina") as saying, "By the year 1754, the horses most regarded in South Carolina for draft or the saddle were known as the Chickasaw breed. This was a stock of horses originally introduced into Florida by the Spanish. They were generally well formed, active and easily kept, but small . . . being remarkable for their muscular development and great endurance; when crossed with the imported Thoroughbred they produced animals of great beauty, strength and fleetness, improving thereby the stock of the country in a very great degree."

The Cherokees and Chickasaws were neighboring tribes inhabiting the lands just north of Spanish Florida. They were for a while a buffer between the French in the west, the Spaniards in the south, and the English in the north, and they traded with all three. The Choctaws and the Creeks ranged a little farther south, but since they were not next to the English, their horses were not obtained as frequently as those of the Cherokees and Chickasaws.

4

their horses had short-horse characteristics. They were described as general utility horses, short and heavily muscled, quick to action, but not distance runners. The same words are used to describe Quarter Horses today. It was not long until blood from England was crossed on these Indian mares and the justly famous Celebrated American Quarter Running Horse was on his way.

If the Galloways of England were sired by a fugitive from the Spanish Armada, they were blood brothers of the Indian ponies of the Southeast. The progenitor of the Narraganset, Old Snipe, was also supposedly a wild horse that one day swam to Point Judith. All of which is to say the Narragansets and Galloways were Spanish or of Spanish descent.

It is most difficult today to say exactly what the Spanish horses were in the fifteenth and sixteenth centuries. It has been customary to speak of them as Barbs or Arabians. Robert Cunninghame Graham is probably as responsible as anyone for this belief since his *Horses of the Conquest*[5] is almost the only popular work on the subject. When one recalls that the Mohammedan or Arabian conquest of Spain came in the year 711 and Moorish rule lasted until the time of Columbus, what could be more natural than to assume that some Arabian blood was brought to the New World by the Spaniards?

Notwithstanding, the evidence seems to indicate that Spanish Barbs, not Arabians, furnished the bulk of the horses imported into the New World. Historians, chroniclers, and poets who lived during the Moorish invasions of Spain speak of the horses as African, Moorish, Barbary, or Tlemcen horses, and not as Arabians. The men were Berbers, Zenetes, and other North Africans. They doubtlessly took their own Barb horses into Spain.

After her occupation, Spain was proud of Barb horses. One of the highest officials imported a superb Barb stallion which became

[5] Robert Bontine Cunninghame Graham, *The Horses of the Conquest*, 119. Cunninghame Graham wrote many books to delight a horseman, especially one interested in Latin America. His mother was Spanish, his father Scottish, and horses his great weakness. He spent considerable time on the American frontier between 1870 to 1890, from Canada to Patagonia. His books are both autobiographical and historical. An American edition of *The Horses of the Conquest* was published by the University of Oklahoma Press in 1949.

5

the fountainhead of the *Guzmanes* and *Valenzuelas*, celebrated strains of *Jinete* horses in Spain.

Prior to the Moorish invasions, a heavier, coarse, and hairy-legged horse had been common in Spain. It had been brought in from France to carry the heavily armored knights. When the Moors settled, they saw little use for these huge animals. They preferred their own horses or smaller native horses which had been in Spain since Roman days.

Southern Spain soon became known as the best horse country, especially the province of Málaga in the old kingdom of Sevilla. This mountainous region, called Ronda, was not too distant from the ports from which the various expeditions left for the New World.[6]

Thus the Quarter Horse is a cross of two equine bloods. One is of Spanish origin, coming from the mountains of Ronda to the southeastern American settlements of the Spaniards in Guale, which extended from Georgia south through Florida. By the time the slower-moving English decided to settle in the New World, the horses were already in the hands of the Indians roaming in our Southeast. From these Indians the American settlers obtained foundation mares for the Quarter Horse. The top line which created the Quarter Horse was obtained from the Hobbies and Galloways imported by the Cavalier settlers of Georgia, Carolina, and Virginia. It was Barb blood spiced with a Celtic infusion and refined with a dash of Eastern blood that fashioned the present-day Quarter Horse.

Ω Ω Ω Ω COLONIAL HORSES

The history of the Quarter Horse during Colonial times is closely related to that of the Thoroughbred. It is impossible to study one without the other. Thoroughbred historians generally believe that their animal is the Colonial Quarter Horse, while Quarter Horse writers have pointed out that there were Quarter Horses in America before there were Thoroughbreds. The answer is, of course, that

[6] For a more extended discussion of Spanish horses see Robert M. Denhardt, *The Horse of the Americas*, 13–24.

6

both had their American beginnings about the same time, and the colonists used both the long- and the short-horse as they wished.

The word "breed" is used loosely to mean an animal capable of reproducing its characteristics. Used strictly, it means an animal registered in a pedigree book. Thus in the strict sense there were no American Quarter Horses until 1940 and, by the same token, no American Thoroughbreds until 1873. In each case private or temporary records had been kept earlier, but the dates given are those of the first official studbooks of the present organizations. The earlier records were useful in compiling the present studbooks, but their existence did not create a breed in either case. Examples of earlier records for the Thoroughbred are Mason, Skinner, and Edgar.[7] Examples of earlier records for the Quarter Horse are Trammel, Lock, and Anson.[8]

Historical fact leaves no doubt that quarter racing was popular in the colonies for more than two hundred years before the Thoroughbred became a breed. There is no question that the horses were called Quarter Horses. These same horses furnish the blood for the horses later registered as American Quarter Horses. These three facts, together with the Quarter Horse's distinct conformation, are the justification for forming a separate breed.

Patrick Nisbett Edgar, born in Ireland, came to America at the turn of the century and settled in Virginia about 1808. According to one story, he killed his father's gardener and fled to America. In any case, he was a popular and welcome visitor at many plantation houses. He died from exposure in a snowstorm in 1857 on the south bank of the Roanoke River. His worn saddlebags, which he

[7] Richard Mason gave his name to *Mason's Farrier* although he only started the ball rolling. This annual was revised and printed for many years by different editors. The original edition appeared in 1814, and in 1828 it contained one of the first registries of the American blood horse. The sixth edition, *The Gentlemen's New Pocket Farrier*, published in 1833, edited by Peter Cottom, was the best. John Stuart Skinner, who was also an editor of *Mason's Farrier*, began his writing career as editor of a farm journal. Patrick Nisbett Edgar compiled the first separate studbook in 1833.

[8] The Trammels and Newmans were well-known horse breeders of Sweetwater, Texas, about the turn of the century. At one time they owned Barney Owens and Dan Tucker, and they bred Pan Zareta. W. W. Lock bought Rondo and made that name a household word in South Texas. William Anson, of the San Angelo region, owned Harmon Baker and Arch Oldham and bred Jim Ned. All kept records, and Anson wrote some of the first and best accounts of the Quarter Horse.

7

kept stuffed with pedigrees and descriptions of the outstanding horses he heard about or saw, are now in the collection of the Virginia Historical Society. His life from childhood revolved around good horseflesh.

Edgar's principal work was *The American Race-Turf Register, Sportsman's Herald and General Stud Book*, which listed pedigrees and descriptions of many Quarter Horses and well over one hundred of their descendants.[9] From the entries, let's select Twigg, one of Janus' great sons, and try to determine whether the description fits the Thoroughbred or the Quarter Horse. (C.A.Q.R.H. means Celebrated American Quarter Running Horse.)

TWIGG

(Goode's old) C.A.Q.R.H. a beautiful bright bay horse, heavily made, with a large blaze face, and two white hind feet, 14 hands 1 inch high, very compact, highly formed and possessed with great muscular powers, symmetry, action and strength.

He was a Quarter of a mile race horse, of the very first class. His speed was unknown to all his competitors, and whenever he was equally matched, he was universally successful. He won immense sums of money and hogsheads of tobacco. We have heard his breeder at different times assert that he was the strongest and the swiftest horse on the universe for three or four hundred yards, and that it was impossible for any horse in existence to beat him unless he was made to carry heavy weights, or run a distance beyond one quarter of a mile. He rarely ever was beaten, unless from some of the foregoing causes. The only horses, in his prime of life, which generally attempted to contend with him, were Polly Williams and Paddy Whack. He ran upwards of a dozen times with each, and newer was beaten but once by each, owing entirely to the weight which he carried, which was generally 108 pounds. He beat Polly Williams 8 times out of nine, for from 80,000 to 100,000 pounds of tobacco. He also beat Paddy Whack 11 times out of 12 for very large sums of money and tobacco. He was run against Paddy Whack at Nicholson's Quarter Race paths, in

9 Edgar's book was to be a two-volume work. Only one volume, published in 1833, appeared. It was printed in New York at the press of Henry Mason, 76 Maiden Lane. The title page listed Edgar's address as Granville County, North Carolina.

Mecklenburgh County, in the State of Virginia, for 80,000 pounds of tobacco, when he beat him ten feet, (with the greatest ease) in one quarter of a mile. He had at two or three different times beaten him for from 30,000 up to 50,000 pounds of tobacco. Another race was made in the year 1786 to be run at the same place for 100,000 pounds of tobacco, Twigg carrying 20 pounds more than Paddy Whack, which was won by the latter, beating him only 18 inches.

He was bred by the late Mr. John Goode, Sen. of Mecklenburgh Co., Va. (commonly called Little Twigg); foaled in 1778.

Got by I. H. Old Janus—C.A.Q.R. mare Puckett's Switch, by I. H. Old Janus—I. H. Old Janus—I. H. Old Janus—I. H. Old Jolly Roger—I. H. Old Monkey. Mecklenburgh Co., Va. April 6th, 1798.

John Goode, Sen.[10]

Of the imported horses, Janus was the greatest sire of Quarter Horses. Not all imported horses were good short-horse sires. Some that did cross and produce sprinters were Bulle-Rock, Jolly Roger, Celer, Morton's Traveler, Mark Anthony, Gimcrack, and Shark.

This background with the descriptions helps us to evaluate the Quarter Horse's position relative to that of the Thoroughbred. A Quarter Horse had sprinting speed; the Thoroughbred, bottom. The Quarter Horse ran 440 yards or less. The Thoroughbred ran one mile (1,760 yards) or more.

Henry William Herbert, writing during the middle of the nineteenth century, says that before Fearnought was imported there was little besides quarter racing in America.[11] Although long races had been run in America before Fearnought, afterwards they became the rule. Thus we have Fearnought, an English race horse, standing on considerable leg, representing the Thoroughbred breeder's ideal—a four-mile horse with enough bottom to run several heats if necessary. The description of Fearnought is not that of a Quarter Horse, but then nobody called Fearnought or any other horse of his caliber a Celebrated American Quarter Horse. Fearnought and others like him were responsible for the Thorough-

10 Edgar, *The American Race-Turf Register*, 508.
11 *Frank Forester's Horse and Horsemanship of the United States*, I, 128.

9

bred, just as Janus and his peers were responsible for the Quarter Horse.

If there was one horse that gave class and distinction to the Colonial Quarter Horse it was the same Janus. John H. Wallace, in his book entitled *The Horse of America*,[12] writes that Janus was the progenitor of a tribe of very fast Quarter Horses and that although Janus did not found that tribe, he improved it.

In *The American Farmer*, quoted in John Stuart Skinner's edition of *Mason's Farrier*, is a word picture of Janus:

> Although Janus partook of every cross in his pedigree calculated for the distance turf horse, yet his stock were more remarkable for speed than bottom. Janus, from his shoulders back, was considered the most perfect formed horse ever seen in Virginia by the most skillful connoisseurs; he was remarkable for roundness of contour, strength of articulation, and indicating great powers and stamina in his whole conformation.
>
> His stock partook of these qualities in an eminent degree, and for thirty or forty years they were considered as a "peculiar stock," as they invariably exhibited, even in the third and fourth generations from the old horse, the same compactness of form, strength and the power. The Janus stock have exceeded all others in the United States for speed, durability and general uniformity of good form.[13]

This is the description of a Quarter Horse, and not of a Thoroughbred, Colonial or modern. The Quarter Horse's shape and reason for existence has not changed. The Quarter Horse needed speed and ruggedness, for he was the average man's all-round horse for use on farm, ranch and track.

Ω Ω Ω Ω HORSES OF THE REVOLUTION

The Quarter Horse played an important part in the Revolutionary

---

[12] Wallace was from Iowa, and was unlucky enough to publish a studbook that was immediately overshadowed by Sanders De Weese Bruce's work, *The American Stud Book*. Wallace then turned to trotters and found a better audience. His last work was *The Horse of America*, which contained his best writings about the race horse in the United States. See also note 18 below.

[13] *The Gentleman's New Pocket Farrier*, 302. This is just one of the many editions of *Mason's Farrier*. See note 7 above.

10

War, and contrariwise the Revolution played an important part in Quarter Horse breeding.

Before the war there were many locations where Quarter Horses were bred, but perhaps the best horses were found in Virginia and the Carolinas. Several campaigns were carried out in these states during the Revolutionary War. Washington and Rochambeau drove south from White Plains, New York, to Yorktown, in southeastern Virginia. Cornwallis sailed to Charleston and Savannah and made several campaigns into the interior, once going as far as Camden and Kings Mountain. The British also drove north out of Wilmington. The brilliant cavalry officer, Sir Banastre Tarleton, raided the South, plundering, burning, and capturing every good horse he could lay his hands on. This movement through the best horse country did not stop until 1781 when Cornwallis surrendered in Virginia and warfare ceased. One can imagine what effect it had on normal breeding programs.

Immediately after the war, racing was resumed in the middle and southern states and west into Tennessee and Kentucky. It thrived when men such as Andrew Jackson gave it attention. In fact, racing was more prevalent after the Revolutionary War than it had been in preceding years. This was true even though the fighting and raids had almost wiped out the breeding stock in some of the older areas. In Virginia, Quarter Horse racing and breeding shifted from the traditional centers along the Rappahannock River to the Roanoke Valley. This valley now became the place where many short-horses had their birth.

J. F. D. Smyth, in his *Tour in the United States of America*, written in 1784, comments:

> In the southern part of the colony [Virginia] and in North Carolina they are much attached to *quarter-racing*, which is always a match between two horses, to run one quarter of a mile straight out; being merely an excursion of speed; and they have a breed that performs it with astonishing velocity, beating every other at that distance with great ease; but they have no bottom. However, I am confident that there is not a horse in England, nor perhaps the whole world, that can excell them in rapid speed.[14]
> 14 See Vol. I, 22–24.

11

The outstanding position occupied by the Virginia southside was not due to ideal surroundings but rather came as a result of the Revolutionary War. The British and the Americans together succeeded in eliminating most of the local blood found in New York, Pennsylvania, the Carolinas, Maryland, and tidewater Virginia. The Roanoke Valley had the good fortune of being practically undisturbed by the war. Here Quarter Horses raced all during the Revolution. They also continued to breed from the old Virginia stock of Jolly Roger, Janus, and Mark Anthony. As Fairfax Harrison says in his delightful book, *The Background of the American Stud Book*, in speaking of the short-horse breeders in the Roanoke Valley:

> When these men sent their promising youngsters on from their local race-fields to be introduced to a larger world on the courses at Petersburg and Richmond and thence at Washington, Annapolis, Long Island and Charleston, and heard the demand for documented as distinguished from traditional pedigrees, they found it as difficult convincingly to respond as they did to adjust themselves to other unaccustomed English conventions. It had been sufficient for them that the dam from which they bred had the reputation of being a "double Janus" or "descended" from Mary Grey.[15]

There are definite Revolutionary War records of horses being stolen or, to use a more modern word, liberated, and then recaptured. There are also records of British soldiers killing horses which they did not need so that the American troops could not have them. If this seems cruel, it should be remembered that horses to armies of the Revolutionary period were not only motorcycles and trucks—they were also the telegraph and radios, tractors, and occasionally even food supply. To both sides, they were essential. Consequently, destroying the animals to keep them out of the hands of the enemy was analogous to cutting communication lines or destroying commissary supplies in modern warfare.

Examples of the destruction of horses for military reasons abound. Three sons of Old Bacchus—two that were rated C.A.Q.R.H.—were captured by the British and drowned in the

[15] See page 20.

York River of Virginia along with the well-known mare Nancy Wake.

Black-and-All-Black, of obvious color, was the property of Sir Peyton Skipwith of Mecklenburg County, Virginia, who sold him to Tucker and Burge for 500,000 pounds of tobacco—thus proving the stallion's value. Lieutenant Colonel Tarleton "liberated" the stallion only to have General Lafayette of the American Army recapture him.

The greatest effect of the war on breeding, however, was the shift of the main breeding centers from the coastal region of the middle and southern colonies to the valleys on the west side of the Appalachian Mountains, away from the dangers of war.

Ω Ω Ω Ω AN ENGLISHMAN DESCRIBES THE QUARTER HORSE

The unique conformation of the Quarter Horse is not something recently developed. When a Steel Dust Quarter Horse stands beside a good Thoroughbred, even the uninitiated can detect the differences. These same qualities were present in the Quarter Horse during the Colonial days.

Early in the 1800's, an Englishman visiting America described the differences between the clean-bred English race horse and the Colonial sprinter:

> I was particularly struck by the fact that the American horse, as compared with the English, was inferior in height of the forehand and in the loftiness and thinness of the withers, and in the setting on, and carriage of the neck and crest, while he was superior in the general development of his hind quarters, in the let down of his hams, and in his height behind, and further remarkable for his formation, approaching to what is often seen in the Irish horse, and known as the goose rump. I still think that these are the prevailing and characteristic differences of the horses of the two countries. I fancy that I can perceive the American racer standing very much higher behind and lower before, than his English congener.[16]

[16] Herbert, *Frank Forester's Horse and Horsemanship*, I, 116. Herbert arrived in America in 1831 and was a well-known and popular writer, especially on hunting and fishing subjects. His book on horses, however, is a must for any serious study of the horse in America.

13

The same differences are present today in the Steel Dust Quarter Horse and the Thoroughbred. The Quarter Horse carries his head low, which makes for sure-footedness in rough going; because of thick layers of muscles, he does not have lofty or thin-peaked withers; he is still superior in muscular development of hindquarters and still "hams down." His tail is somewhat lower than the point of the hips, and he stands higher behind than in front. Such description of type, that has remained consistent for almost two hundred years, speaks well for the breed and, indeed, points up characteristics that create his utility. These are the same characteristics which the infusion of too much English (Thoroughbred) blood will destroy.

In addition to Janus, an outstanding Quarter Horse sire of the Colonial era was Old Peacock, who lived from 1760 to 1786. He was a son of Janus and listed in the early editions of *The American Stud Book*[17] as a Celebrated Quarter Horse. Another outstanding horse was Goode's Babram, who was born in 1766 and died in 1789. Babram was an inbred Janus and was known as the fastest Quarter Horse of his day. He died at the age of twenty-three, during a quarter race match for five hundred Spanish dollars over the famous "Lewis Paths" in Mecklenburg County, Virginia. He was matched against a challenger named Juniper who was passing through the county and who was also by Janus. Babram was well ahead when he crossed his front legs and fell, breaking his neck. If Cunninghame Graham were writing this, he would add that

---

[17] *The American Stud Book* was started by Sanders Bruce, who wrote the first seven volumes. Volume I was issued in 1868 and covered horses from A to K. Later Bruce decided to make some changes, and to insure that everyone would buy the new Volume I, he included horses A to L. Consequently the first edition became useless. The new volume was issued in 1873. Volume II was also published in 1873, Volume III in 1882, Volume IV in 1884, Volume V in 1887, and Volume VI in 1894. Bruce compiled Volume VII of the series but sold his rights to the Jockey Club, which published Volume VII in 1898. Through most of the nineties, the Jockey Club had been trying to gain possession of Bruce's work. The fight was long and bitter and went to court, with Bruce winning in lower court. However, the Jockey Club appealed, and although the case never went to final judgment, the litigation had so exhausted Bruce's finances that he settled out of court for $35,000. Thus all volumes of *The American Stud Book* after Volume VI carry the imprint of the Jockey Club. Only the first seven volumes are of particular interest to Quarter Horse breeders and historians, because the Appendix maintained by Bruce, listing Quarter Horses, was dropped by the Jockey Club. See Chapter 2, note 1 below.

Babram would have preferred to go the way he did, to whatever heaven there is for horses, doing what he loved most—racing.[18]

The third exceptional Quarter Horse was Meade's Celer, who was born in 1766 and who died in 1804. He, too, was by Janus. Two others that should be mentioned are Old Twigg (1770–90) and Goode's Brimmer (1776–86). The first was by Janus, the second by Harris Eclipse. All were celebrated short-horses of their day.

Although the Quarter Horse lost some of his popularity in the East at the beginning of the nineteenth century, there were breede·s farther west who continued raising short-horses. The closing years of the eighteenth century, then, marked the end of the period in which the best Quarter Horses were raised along the Atlantic Seaboard. Now Kentucky, Tennessee, Missouri, and Illinois replace Virginia and the Carolinas as the principal breeding centers for the short-horse.

---

18 The account of Babram's race with Old Jupiter can be found in Edgar's *American Race-Turf Register*, 98. In *Wallace's American Stud-Book*, 46, Wallace errs in calling Goode's Babram "Babraham." Bruce, on the other hand, spells his name correctly in his *American Stud Book*, I, 894, and adds that Babram was the best and fastest "quarter-horse" of his day. Wallace also says he was highly distinguished as a "quarter racer."

Wallace was from Ohio, and he was able to do something that the horsemen along the Atlantic Seaboard had never been able to do—bring together the pedigree material of the American blood horse, and print it. Wallace, however, printed only one volume. Three factors worked against him. First, he was not critical enough of the material he collected; secondly, he used a system of listing which was different from that to which the breeders were accustomed; and lastly, Bruce, who was doing a more acceptable job, published his first volume before Wallace was able to make any corrections or issue another volume.

2. THE QUIET YEARS

ΩΩΩΩ The Movement West

SHORT RACING along the Atlantic Coast went out of favor at the beginning of the 1800's and since that time the records, located in the East, of the Thoroughbred breeders contain very little information about the Quarter Horse. Short-horse men were found after 1800 in Kentucky, Missouri, Ohio, Illinois, Tennessee, Arkansas, Louisiana, and Texas. Many horsemen in these areas were not interested in four-mile horses. They wanted speed, not bottom; they were looking for sprinters, not "stayers." Many kept records of their breeding. It is to their records we now turn for information.

At the county fairs in the agricultural communities and on the frontier half-mile tracks, Quarter Horses and Thoroughbreds still met occasionally. As a result records of some Quarter Horses can be found in the Appendices of *The American Stud Book*, listed for racing purposes only but with valuable pedigree information,[1] among the most authentic available. Other pedigree information was to be found in folders distributed to advertise popular Quarter Horses standing at stud. In addition, a number of turf magazines of the era—such as *The American Turf Register and Sporting Magazine* and *Spirit of the Times*[2]—carried many stories about Quarter Horses and their pedigrees.

[1] An appendix to *The American Stud Book* was introduced by Bruce in Volume I, and subsequent books compiled by Bruce, through Volume VII, contained one. Bruce said pedigrees of all horses, mares, and geldings reported too late for classification, and those whose dams had no names and whose pedigrees were not authenticated as Thoroughbred, were included and published as reported to the author. Regardless of his reasons for publication, the material is invaluable to the Quarter Horse historian, because it changes many legendary horses, such as Steel Dust, Shiloh, Billy, and Cold Deck, into flesh and blood.

[2] Although there were other magazines and newspapers that carried some race horse material, by far the most productive for the Quarter Horse historian are these

16

Almost as soon as Kentucky and Tennessee were settled, short-horse men began bringing in their horses; in fact, some arrived carrying the first pioneers. Excellent stock from Virginia, Maryland, and the Carolinas was brought in, representing Janus, Jolly Roger, Morton's Traveler, and other great sprinting sires. Janus blood was preferred. Will Williams, one of the outstanding breeders, wrote from his farm near Nashville in 1856: "The early stallions here, of the Janus family, were—Jupiter, said to be a son—Cross's; Comet, Lewis's, son of Harry Hill's Janus, and said to have a Marc Anthony and Jolly Roger cross; Sterne, Blakemore's; and Bowie's horse, who took his owner's name, pronounced Biu-ey. His colts are said to have been unequaled as Quarter Horses."[3] A little farther on, he says: "Contemporary with him of the Sir Archy stock, stood, at Summers, Grey Archy, Timoleon, and Pacific."[4]

Will Williams also make an interesting statement concerning Brimmer, who is found in many Quarter Horse pedigrees: "As to Brimmer, my father bought Eclipse, about the close of the Revolution, of Colonel Harris, and he stated that Eclipse was the sire of Col. Goode's Brimmer." Williams rates the greatest sire of Quarter Horses as follows: "Janus, ch. by Janus, Old Fox, Bald Galloway;

---

two. *The American Turf Register* was founded and edited by John Stuart Skinner, who published it for six years. The next four years saw two editors, Allen Jones Davie and Gideon B. Smith. The next editor, from 1840 to 1844, was the incomparable William Trotter Porter. Porter himself was never an expert horseman, he was much too fond of angling, but as a news reporter of a racing age, he has had no equal. His reports of the matches between Wagner and Grey Eagle and of Boston and Fashion are in a class by themselves. *The Spirit of the Times* was all Porter's. He founded it and was its editor until 1850, when he withdrew. The last editor of *The Spirit* was E. E. Jones. In all, thirty-one volumes were published. Curiously enough, another racing journal entitled *Porter's Spirit of the Times* was founded in 1856 by one George Wilkes. Seven volumes of this magazine were published.

3 Herbert, *Frank Forester's Horse and Horsemanship, etc.* I, 140. Will Williams was one of the most knowledgeable horsemen who lived during the last quarter of the eighteenth century and the first of the nineteenth. He was born in North Carolina the year the Revolutionary War broke out. He attended law school and then migrated west to settle down in Popular Grove, Tennessee. This area was soon to become a horse-raising center and a racing hot spot for that part of the United States. As a young man growing up in the Roanoke Valley, he personally knew many great horses. Some were sons of Janus—such as Meade's Celer and Old Twigg. In Tennessee he wrote for agricultural journals and carried on a small breeding program of his own. His last two major literary contributions were two long letters written to and for Herbert, who was then writing his *Horse and Horsemanship*, from which the Will Williams' quotations are taken.

4 *Ibid.*, I, 142.

produced the fleetest, then and since known, as quarter horses—quarter mile racers."[5]

Most short-horse blood entered Ohio from Pennsylvania and Virginia. John Van Meter was one of the first to bring good horses to the Scioto Valley region from Virginia. One of the first well-known stallions was Spread Eagle, who traced back through Morton's Traveler to a Spanish mare. There were also Janus and Diomed stock, and in Fairfield County Printer developed a name for himself and his offspring as outstanding "Quarter nags—good in a short race."

In the second or third decade of the nineteenth century, still another famous sire arrived in Ohio, known as Kentucky Whip. Into the Scioto Valley, also from Kentucky, came some Bertrand stock. Eclipse bloodlines were popular in Highland County with Governor Allen Trimble as the principal exponent. About 1825, several stallions came into western Ohio from Kentucky. They were by Cook and Blackburn's Whip. In the early 1800's, fall race meetings were held at Cincinnati, Chillicothe, Dayton, and Hamilton.

Michigan was not long in developing Quarter Horses, many of them coming from New York, Vermont, and Kentucky. Soon after Michigan became a state, Governor Porter brought in Kippalo by John Richards by Sir Archy. Writing of early Michigan horses in the middle 1800's, A. Y. Moore said:

> There are many good horses in the state, called the Bacchus stock, got by Old Bacchus of Ohio, owned by Cone, who was shot at a race track . . . . They are the fastest horses for short races that have even been in our state, not large generally, but very strong and muscular . . . . My neighbor, Mr. Armstrong, owns a horse well known in this state as John Bacchus, as good a half-mile horse as I ever saw. His dam was a "Printer." "Telegraph" . . . is a full brother to John Bacchus, and said to be equally fast. It is said he can run 80 rod in 27 seconds.[6]

Tracks founded in early Michigan were located at Detroit, Ad-

5 *Ibid.*, I, 145–46.
6 *Ibid.*, II, 89–90. Eighty rods are two furlongs or one-fourth of a mile.

18

rian, Cold Water (principally for match races), Kalamazoo (with a two-thirds of a mile straightaway), Marshall, and Jackson.

Kentucky, Tennessee, Ohio, and Michigan are important because it was from these states that the Quarter Horse found its way into Arkansas, Missouri, and Illinois, and then on into Texas, Oklahoma, and Kansas.

Ω Ω Ω Ω SIR ARCHY AND PRINTER

The most important stallion to influence the Quarter Horse after the Colonial Janus was that Thoroughbred son of Diomed, Sir Archy. This great stallion produced 135 descendants listed by John Stuart Skinner in *Mason's Farrier and Stud Book*. In many ways, his importance in Quarter Horse bloodlines is surprising since he was a large horse from the short-horse man's point of view, standing 16 hands, and because his best times were made on the four-mile tracks. Yet his blood, when crossed with the Quarter mares, left little to be desired. He had more influence lineage-wise than any other horse during the transition period.

Sir Archy was foaled in 1805. He was sired by Diomed (1777–1813), who was imported into Virginia in 1798. Diomed's sire was Florizel by King Herod by Tarter. Florizel's dam was by Cygnet and out of Cartouch, whose dam was Ebony, a daughter of Flying Childers. Sir Archy's dam was imported Castianira by Rockingham out of Tabitha.

Just as Janus dominated the Quarter Horse during the period from 1746 to 1800, so Sir Archy and his offspring seem to have dominated the transition period from 1800 to 1850.

As happens in the case of many great horses, there were a few people who questioned Sir Archy's breeding. Rumor gives the credit to the stallion Gabriel, sire of Post Boy, Harlequin, and Oscar. However, Colonel Tayloe and Colonel Randolph, who took Castianira to Diomed to be bred, clearly stated in a letter to John Skinner[7] that Diomed was Sir Archy's sire. As Henry William

---

[7] This letter is quoted in *The American Farmer*, IX, 143. This journal started out as strictly a farm publication, but before long it included a section entitled "Sporting Olio," which included racing information and pedigrees.

19

Herbert observed, what stallion then so worthy to be the sire of Sir Archy as Diomed?[8]

In the spring of 1804, when Sir Archy was bred, Diomed was standing at the farm of one Colonel Seldens, situated a few miles below Richmond. Seldens' son, when interviewed by Herbert, said that he saw Castianira covered by Diomed.

Sir Archy was a beautiful all bay horse, except for a white right hind foot. He stood 16 hands high and showed great power and substance. Although he did not run a great many times for that day and age, he ran enough to beat all of the outstanding racers of the day. When he retired, he had no equal on the turf.

In the *American Turf Register* of 1841, a writer, signing himself "Observer,"[9] declared that for renown, both on the turf and in the stud, none but Sir Archy deserved to be regarded as the American "Highflyer."

We find that many of the greatest short-horse sires of the nineteenth century, such as Cold Deck, Shiloh, and Billy, trace back to Sir Archy. Even two of the best of the twentieth-century sires, Old Joe Bailey and Peter McCue, are descendants of Sir Archy. Old Joe Bailey traces three times on his dam's side and three times on his sire's side to Sir Archy. The Shilohs trace directly to Sir Archy. Shiloh was by Union by Van Tromp by Big Solomon by Sir Solomon by Sir Archy. The same can be said for the Billys, who are a branch of the Shilohs. The Steel Dusts trace to Sir Archy also. Steel Dust was by Harry Bluff out of Big Nance, who was by Timoleon by Sir Archy.

Perhaps the most influential horse after Sir Archy affecting the development of the Quarter Horse during this period was Printer. *The American Stud Book* gives the sire of Printer as imported Janus, which seems impossible since imported Janus died in 1780. Printer died in 1828. His sire was probably a son of Janus—unless

---

8 *Frank Forester's Horse and Horsemanship*, I, 172.

9 It was commonly accepted among the various writers on equine subjects during the early nineteenth century that only Benjamin Ogle Tayloe (1796–1868) would write for the sporting journals under the name "Observer." As Wallace pointed out in the introduction of his *American Stud-Book*, Tayloe was recognized for over a quarter of a century by this signature. For more on *American Turf Register*, see note 2 above. For more on Tayloe see note 4, Chapter 3.

imported Janus lived to the unlikely age of forty-seven years. Colonel Sanders Bruce, editor of the first volumes of *The American Stud Book*, referred to Printer. Under Printer's name are these familiar words: "He was a Quarter Horse."[10]

Printer was a great sire, and some of the best present-day Quarter Horses trace to him. Printer was the grandsire of Bay Cold Deck by Hamburg Dick; Grasshopper, the dam of Rolling Deck, and Doe Belly, was out of a daughter of Printer. Boanerges, a son of Printer, sired Monkey around 1836; she in turn produced Munch Meg by Alford, granddam of Nannie Reap and Butt Cut. Old Dan and Comet were also Printer Quarter Horses. Tiger, the brown horse that raced in Indiana, was a grandson of Printer. Mary Cook, a daughter of Printer, produced Dan Secres by Joe Chalmers, who also was the sire of Nelly Grey. Nelly Grey produced the famous Mittie Stephens in 1869 when she was bred to young Shiloh. Mittie Stephens was the dam of the original Rondo who was owned by W. W. Lock. She was also the dam of Shelby, General Ross, Sallie Johnson, Dead Cinch, and Heeley.

The Printer family contributed to several of the present-day families through a second stallion known as Printer. This Printer (1872–92) was by Old Cold Deck by Old Billy, and out of a granddaughter of Printer, from whom he derived his name. Missouri Mike and Jeff were by this Printer. Missouri Mike was the sire of Little Earl and, according to one report, a great-grandsire of Old Fred. Old Red Buck's dam, Pet Dawson, was by Jeff out of Old Babe by Little Earl. Printer was a half brother of Barney Owens, Diamond Deck, and Berry's Cold Deck.

The Tiger blood, so important in the founding of the Sykes Rondo family, came from Tiger (1812–32), who was by Blackburn's Whip out of Jane Hunt.

Blackburn's Whip, according to Wallace's *American Stud Book*, was often called Kentucky Whip. He was born in 1805 and died in 1828. He was sired by imported Whip, who was by Saltram by Cartouch by Sebright's Arabian. Whip's dam was by Herod. Blackburn's Whip's dam was Spreckleback by Celer by Janus.

10 Vol. II, 566.

Blackburn's Whip contributed greatly to the Steel Dust family. Harry Bluff, the sire of Steel Dust, was by Short Whip by Blackburn's Whip.

The Copper Bottom family was established in 1832 by Copper Bottom. This was only five years after the final establishment of the English Thoroughbred. Copper Bottom was a chestnut horse, foaled in 1828, bred by Edward Parker, Lancaster, Pennsylvania, and brought to Texas in 1839 by General Sam Houston. Copper Bottom was sired by Sir Archy and was out of a daughter of imported Buzzard and the Rattle Mare by Rattle. On his dam's side, Copper Bottom traces twice to imported Janus.[11]

General Sam Houston shipped Copper Bottom by water to New Orleans, Louisiana, and from there to Galveston, Texas. From Galveston, Copper Bottom was taken to Chambers County and later to Huntsville, Walker County, and on to Sulphur Springs in Hopkins County, where he died in 1860. Copper Bottom left colts around Galveston that set records all along the beach, and many modern breeders have Copper Bottom blood in their string. Some account of Copper Bottom's progeny has also been kept in *The American Stud Book*. For example, in the Appendix to Volume VII is an entry for Margaret W, a brown mare foaled in 1890, bred and owned by George H. Williams, of Paris, Texas, which adjoins Hopkins County. Her dam traces directly to Copper Bottom.

By the latter half of the nineteenth century, Quarter Horse breeding and Quarter Horse pedigrees can be verified with considerable accuracy. In many respects, the next period in Quarter Horse history can be called the Golden Era, since this period between 1850 and 1900 saw Shiloh, Steel Dust, Old Billy, Cold Deck, Missouri Mike, and Barney Owens in their heyday, with others such as Dan Tucker, Little Steve, Old Fred, Peter McCue, Rondo, and Traveler coming on the scene.

---

[11] *The Quarter Horse Breeder*, 105–24. Helen Michaelis, in this book edited by M. H. Lindeman, makes an excellent survey of all of the important early Quarter Horse families.

3. LEGENDARY HEROES

Hɪsᴛᴏʀʏ has never been an exact science even though by definition it began with written records. John H. Wallace said that
in no other department of human knowledge has there been such a
universal and persistent habit of misrepresenting the truth as in
matters relating to the horse.[1] John Stuart Skinner wrote that
contradictions and discrepancies "were not included with the inten-
tion of disputing any reliable person's words or of belittling any
horse." Then he quoted an old chronicle which said, "Men may
forget, and forgetting deny that such things were."[2] There are
very few written records covering the Quarter Horse since the
middle of the nineteenth century. For this reason the accounts
found in the next few chapters, which came to me mostly by word
of mouth, may vary somewhat from accounts found elsewhere.

The story as told here was gathered, generally speaking, by
either Helen Michaelis or me. Between the two of us, we corre-
sponded with, or talked to, most of the Quarter Horse owners, or
their descendants, who were active between 1850 and 1940. We
did find that there was often little agreement on some items, even
between fathers, sons, uncles, or brothers. Further, an individual
would alter his story somewhat as the years passed, or as he was
talking to one or the other of us.

However, many of our informants were especially helpful, such
as Mrs. William Anson, Coke Blake, Ott Adams, Dan Casement,
W. W. Lock, George Clegg, Coke Roberds, and Walter Trammel.
Ed Bateman, Sr., also deserves credit as he and J. M. Huffington

[1] *The Horse of America*, 94.
[2] *American Turf Register and Sporting Magazine*, VII, Allen J. Davie, ed., 9, 393.

were responsible for the remarkably valuable little magazine known as *The Quarter Horse*.[3]

Even if some of the following details are not completely accurate, it matters little. The important thing is that there were such horses as Steel Dust. They lived, worked, ran, and begot sons and daughters, and founded a mighty race, the American Quarter Horse.

Ω Ω Ω Ω Steel Dust (1843)

The Thoroughbred and the Quarter Horse have always been closely related, even though they have distinctive differences. In Colonial days the popular runners were the sprinters, and when the first American movement for a studbook began, the early chroniclers, such as Tayloe, Skinner, and Edgar,[4] naturally included some of the best Quarter Horses. In addition to these early records, when *The American Stud Book* was first organized, it had an appendix in which the pedigrees of many prominent Quarter Horses such as Steel Dust could be traced.

Steel Dust was the first of the legendary heroes of the modern Quarter Horse world. His sire was Harry Bluff, a son of Short Whip and a Thoroughbred mare named Big Nance, of Timoleon stock. Timoleon was by Sir Archy.

[3] *The Quarter Horse* is the name of the valuable little magazine published by the National Quarter Horse Breeders Association. This magazine was originally granted a second class permit at Knox City, Texas, home of its first, and best editor, Ed Bateman, Sr. Bateman had a gift for writing, and his series entitled "Pecos Bill, Jr." is western humor at its best. However, the features of greatest interest are the stories on foundation animals and the records of short races. When the first issue appeared in April, 1946, it was printed on newsprint, cut size 7½x10. Bateman was editor until January, 1948, at which time two names appeared as editors, C. H. Moss and Dale Graham. Beginning in November of 1948 a new editor appeared, David J. Woodlock. What was happening was that when Bateman gave up the editorship, the secretary of the NQHBA was vainly trying to find a replacement and having to do most of the work himself. The secretary of the NQHBA throughout its brief but stormy career was J. M. Huffington of Hockley and Houston, Texas. Beginning in August of 1949, the name of one of the office girls, E. E. Kingsbury, appeared on the masthead as editor and stayed there until the magazine was discontinued with Volume IV, number 7, October, 1949. Complete files of this little magazine are all but impossible to obtain.

[4] The Tayloe mentioned is Benjamin Ogle Tayloe who was born in 1796 and died in 1868. His grandfather was the last owner of Morton's Traveler. He collected pedigrees for many years and finally wrote a history of the American turf which was published by Skinner in *American Turf Register*, beginning in 1832. For more information on Skinner see note 7, Chapter 1.

Steel Dust was foaled about 1843 in Kentucky. He was brought into Texas by Middleton Perry and Jones Greene in 1844. They settled down near the present site of Lancaster in what is now Dallas County. Steel Dust matured into a stallion a little over 15 hands in height and weighing about 1,200 pounds. He soon had a reputation for speed.

North of Lancaster in Collin County there was also a fast horse, by the name of Monmouth. He, too, was from Kentucky. A race was matched between the two horses, to be run at McKinney. It was a slam-bang event, with even the judicial courts in town closing down so that everyone could attend. In the neighboring towns of Sherman and Jefferson all business come to a standstill. So many people showed up that the main hotel in McKinney, the Foote House, was turned over to the ladies, and the men slept wherever they could. Everything that wasn't nailed down went home with Steel Dust when he won from the favorite, Monmouth.[5]

Several other big races followed—one against Brown Dick, who was owned by Alfred Bailes; another against Shiloh, who was owned by Jack Batchler. Shiloh was another sire who was to make a marked impression on the breed. The race against Shiloh was scheduled to be held on the outskirts of Dallas in 1855, where one of the best short tracks for match races was located. The track was especially desirable because it was laned. Steel Dust, in his eagerness for the race, reared up against the starting chute, broke one of the boards, and ran a piece of it into his shoulder. He never raced again, and the question of which horse was faster—Shiloh or Steel Dust—was never to be settled. Steel Dust forfeited the race, but both stallions went on to fame as foundation Quarter Horse sires.

Jack Batchler, even though he thought his Shiloh the better horse, had unlimited admiration for Steel Dust, and bred many Shiloh fillies to him. One of the better-known progeny of Steel Dust was Tom Driver. Tom Driver was the sire of Shelby, who in turn sired the well-known Pid Hart, the sire of Rocky Mountain Tom. A

---

[5] The story of Steel Dust is best told by Wayne Gard in his attractive little volume entitled *Fabulous Quarter Horse Steel Dust*. It has an adequate Bibliography on pages 51–60 for those wishing to read more about Steel Dust.

fast Steel Dust filly was Grey Alice, the pride of Jim Brown, sheriff of Lee County.

The story of Grey Alice's race with Hildreth's Red Morocco is a classic as told by Sam Hildreth.[6] A big iron kettle was dragged upside down along the prairie to scrape the grass clean for the lanes. A railing was run out between the lanes for some eighty yards. The horses were given a sixteen-foot score and brought up to the line and started by the "ask and answer" method. When the race was over, Grey Alice had won, and more fast fillies were due to call on Steel Dust.

Some of Steel Dust's better-known get were Ram Cat, Jack Traveler, Old Dutchman, Cold Deck, Tom Driver, and Mounts. Peter McCue traces to Steel Dust by way of Dan Tucker's dam. Sykes Rondo was by McCoy Billy by Old Billy who was out of Ram Cat who was by Steel Dust. Old Joe Bailey of Weatherford traces to Steel Dust on both sides. His sire, Eureka, was a grandson of Tom Driver, who was by Steel Dust, and a great-grandson of Mounts, who was also by Steel Dust. Joe Bailey's dam was Susie McQuirter, who was·a granddaughter of Old Dutchman and of Barney, a great-granddaughter of Old Rondo, and a great-great-granddaughter of Old Billy.

Steel Dust contributed to all of the modern Quarter Horse families, especially to the Billy, Cold Deck, Rondo, and Peter McCue strains.

Steel Dust lived the rest of his life on the farm near Lancaster. The Civil War did not affect his popularity, but it did send Mid Perry, his owner, away in 1862. Steel Dust died on Ten Mile Creek some time after 1864 and was buried there on Mid Perry's farm.

In conformation, Steel Dusts were typical Quarter Horses, except that they exhibited what seemed to be unusually large jaws. This impression was created by the fact that their flat disk-shaped jawbones tilted out as well as down. The characteristic could be

---

[6] This interesting episode is described fully in *The Spell of the Turf* written by Samuel C. Hildreth. Sam's father, Vince, was a short-horse man who was perhaps best known for the race in which he matched his horse Red Morocco against Grey Alice, a daughter of Steel Dust. Sam Hildreth spent his life as a trainer of Thoroughbreds.

observed much more clearly when looking at the horse head on rather than from the side. William Anson said the stallions especially were heavy jawed.[7] Dan Casement wrote that their massive jaws seemed to serve as a fitting symbol for the tenacity and determination which marked the Steel Dust strain. He added that they made a strange contrast to the small ears that characterized the breed.[8] This contrast is still noticeable in many of the better Quarter Horses.

The years between the Mexican War and the Civil War (largely the 1850's) saw the introduction of widespread cattle raising in the Great Plains, especially in Texas. Following the Civil War there was a surplus of cattle roaming the Texas area and a shortage of fresh meat in the eastern and northern markets. It was around 1868 that the long drives began, taking vast herds of Texas cattle and horses as far north as Canada. The cow horse was essential to the cattle business, but the small but sinewy mustangs did not fill the eye of the Texas cattlemen. Steel Dust Quarter Horse progeny did, and they furnished the blood for many horses ridden north and west, even to California, out of Texas. With the cattle, Quarter Horse strains were established on ranches throughout the western half of the United States. And thus the legend of Steel Dust followed the Texas cowman.

Ω Ω Ω Ω SHILOH (1844)

The great stallion Shiloh was foaled in Tennessee in 1844 and brought to Texas in 1849 by Jack Batchler. Old Shiloh was by Van Tromp by Thomas' Big Solomon by Sir Solomon by the foundation sire Sir Archy.

The influence of Shiloh is seen especially in the family strains of Billy, Rondo, and Joe Bailey. The Billy family was created by Old Billy, a son of Shiloh. Both of the Rondos were grandsons of Billy. Old Joe Bailey descended twice on his sire's side and twice on his dam's side from Shiloh.

[7] Anson in the May, 1910, issue of *Breeders' Gazette* describes the Quarter Horse in one of the earliest magazine articles to appear on the breed in America.

[8] "Steel Dusts as I Have Known Them," The *American Hereford Journal*, June, 1927.

27

Some of Shiloh's most famous progeny were Young Shiloh, or Shiloh, Jr., Old Billy, Little Jeff Davis, Mammoth, Bay Fanny Bailes, and Grey Fanny Bailes.

Shiloh is a somewhat better-known figure than Steel Dust, his contemporary and competitor. Jack Batchler bought him as a colt and took him to Texas when he moved west to the Lone Star State. The colt grew up into a handsome horse and soon established a reputation as a short-horse.

Batchler finally settled down permanently in 1855 on a farm along the southern edge of Dallas County. There he became acquainted with Jones Greene and Mid Perry, who had moved there from Illinois. They owned Steel Dust.

Batchler went with Greene and Perry to McKinney when they matched Monmouth. Even then he had in mind a match race between his horse Shiloh and their horse Steel Dust. As has been related, the match was finally arranged but never run because of the accident that befell Steel Dust.

Shiloh's reputation was widespread, and many horsemen came to breed their mares to the stallion. According to the records kept by Jack Batchler, the sixties were Shiloh's biggest years at stud. Unfortunately for the modern Quarter Horse historian, Batchler's records seldom mentioned the name of the mare, and almost never mentioned the foal—just the name of the man bringing the mare and the amount paid. Among the men bringing mares to Shiloh between 1860 and 1865 were Mid Perry, I. G. Nelson, W. C. Smith, Thomas Howell, Allen Demoney, and Carter Smith. According to Wayne Gard, who is the best source of information on Steel Dust and Shiloh, Batchler also bred at least one filly to Steel Dust.

Shiloh lived until he reached the age of thirty. He might have lived longer, but one day when Batchler was away Shiloh managed to get into a corral with another stallion and was kicked so badly that he never recovered. He was buried in the pasture next to the house. Batchler was living at that time on Bear Creek, Ellis County, near Bluff Springs.

Jack Batchler's son, Harry, followed in his father's footsteps.

28

He raised Tom Driver, a son of Mammoth by Steel Dust. By 1875 he had left short-horses and was running Thoroughbreds. Harry Batchler never forgot his earlier days of short racing. Wayne Gard says that Henry (Harry) Batchler, in his later years in Dallas, looked back longingly to Shiloh and the other fleet Quarter Horses he had known in his youth.[9] In 1922, Batchler recalled Shiloh the best horse he ever saw, adding that he had seen Steel Dust. He described Shiloh as a stallion that could go like a "rush telegram over a downhill wire."

Wayne Gard's nostalgic reflection on Steel Dust and Shiloh is well worth repeating here:

> The former haunts of Steel Dust still are horse country. On stormy nights some of those who live on Ten Mile Creek may think they hear his whinny—and an answering neigh from Old Shiloh on Bear Creek. If the two stallions could break away from their equine Valhalla, undoubtedly they would come back some night and finish that race of 1855, and thus settle for all time the question of which was the fleeter.[10]

Ω Ω Ω Ω OLD BILLY (1860)

Billy, with his breeding, could hardly help being a legendary figure. He was sired by Shiloh. Old Billy's dam was Ram Cat, a daughter of Steel Dust and Fanny Wolf. So Old Billy, who was sometimes called Billy, Billy Boy, or Billy Fleming, was a Shiloh–Steel Dust cross. He was, in fact, so good that he established the Quarter Horse in South Texas, and gave it the name "Land of the Billys."

Old Billy had quite an interesting history.[11] He received his

[9] Just as Wayne Gard is the outstanding authority on Steel Dust, so too he is the best on Shiloh. Three of his articles on Shiloh are "When Texas Shouted for Shiloh," *Western Horseman*, August, 1949; "Hoofbeats of Old Shiloh," *Cattleman*, September, 1953; and "New Light on Old Shiloh," *Quarter Horse Journal*, December, 1955.

[10] *Fabulous Quarter Horse Steel Dust*, 56.

[11] About thirty years ago there was some confusion about Billy. Much of it was started in an article by J. Frank Dobie, *The Cattleman*, March, 1937. Dobie had talked to Onie Sheeran of Cotulla, Texas, and Onie had told Dobie what he, Onie, believed to be a true story. When Dobie's article appeared I went to Dobie, and obtained a letter of introduction to Onie in order to talk with him about Billy. Onie confirmed the story he told to Dobie, so I spent some more time and went to see Ott Adams, George Clegg, Raymond Dickson, and Alonzo Taylor, all Quarter Horse men who

name from his second owner, William B. "Billy" Fleming of Belmont, Texas. William Fleming was an Indian fighter with the Rangers on the Texas frontier. He also fought in the Confederate Army, was wounded, and as a result he could not write. He could only scribble after a fashion with his left hand, so he kept no records except a few which he dictated to interested breeders and then signed with a scribble. Billy was kept chained to a tree while his original owner fought in the Civil War. When it was over and Fleming bought Billy, the horse was in sorry shape. His hoofs were so long they had to be sawed off, and the scar from the chain on his neck was never lost, nor did that area ever grow hair again.

The mare that did the most for Fleming, when she was crossed by Old Billy, was Paisana. Paisana was a little seal-brown mare raised by Oliver and Bailes of Seguin, Texas. She was a race mare and had been sired by Brown Dick, a son of Berkshire, and she was out of Belton Queen, a daughter of Guinea Boar. Brown Dick, her sire, had quite a short-horse reputation, being undefeated until he met Steel Dust. Steel Dust had been borrowed by Jack Batchler from Mid Perry for this race. Steel Dust won but knew he had been in a race.

The first stallion Fleming got from Old Billy and Paisana was Anthony. He was foaled in 1856. He sired Billy Dribble, Alex Gardner (so named after his owner), Little John Moore, Fashion, Lemonade, and Pink Reed. Billy Dribble sired the Nixon mare that was the sire of Joe Bailey of Gonzales. Fashion and Lemonade were full sisters and campaigned together for several years. Fashion broke the record for three-eighths of a mile at San Angelo when she ran it in thirty-four seconds. In 1893, Lemonade ran four and one-half furlongs in New Orleans in fifty-seven seconds.

Some other foals of Old Billy were Jenny Oliver, Rover, Dora, Sweet Lip, Little Brown Dick, Pancho, Joe Collins, Brown Billy, and McCoy Billy, and some old-timers claimed that Bob Wade was by Old Billy.

were familiar with Billy horses, and all more active in short-horse circles than Onie. The story of Billy as told in this chapter, a composite, is the one generally accepted by Helen Michaelis and me as correct, and agrees for the most part with notes made by me on the South Texas trip made in 1937. See *Denhardt Files*, Billy Horse Folder.

Little Brown Dick sired the dams of Little Ben and Aury. Little Ben was bred to Aury and the foal was Suzie McQuirter, dam of Weatherford's Joe Bailey. Pancho was a light-brown horse foaled in 1884. Alex Gardner paid Fleming $1,500 for Pancho, Joe Collins, and Dora. Joe Collins ended up in the hands of Clay McGonigle and proved to be a great sire, producing Blue Gown and Buck Shot. Pancho was open to the world and if he was ever beaten it was kept real quiet, and Helen Michaelis could not find out about it. Pancho died of lockjaw from a nail puncture about 1890. He sired many colts, but the most famous was Jim Ned, whom William Anson bought. Dan Casement bought a Jim Ned colt which he called Balleymooney. Balleymooney sired Red Dog, Frosty, Colleen, Clipper, Billy Byrne, and many others.

McCoy Billy by Old Billy sired Sykes Rondo. Sykes Rondo sired Jenny, dam of Little Joe, Baby Ruth, dam of Paul El, and Nettie Harrison, Kittie II, Blue Eyes, and many more. Jenny was also the dam of King, who became known as Possum in Arizona.

Billy Fleming's Billy horse developed into one of Texas' greatest assets. Fleming deserves much of the credit. About 1888 he quit the racing circuit but continued raising and selling horses. In 1907, at the age of seventy-seven, he sold the last of his Billy horses, six mares and Little John Moore, to Fred Matthies of Seguin. Unhappy without his horses, he followed them to Seguin and lived at the Matthies' place until his death on April 30, 1911.

Ω Ω Ω Ω COLD DECK (1862)

Cold Deck was described in one pedigree circular as being the "Boss Quarter Horse in America." The only person with whom I talked who knew Old Cold Deck was Coke Blake,[12] and though some of the details do not fit perfectly with other information, on the whole what he told me is probably correct. Coke Blake said that his idea of the perfect Quarter Horse was formed when he was

---

12 I spent a couple of days visiting with Coke Blake in Oklahoma in 1939. The Blake horse today has faded into other more popular lines, but fifty years ago it was one of the most popular short-horse bloodlines in Oklahoma and Arkansas. I went to Van Buren after leaving Coke, but I could not uncover any reliable information on Cold Deck. See *Denhardt Files*, Blake Folder.

31

privileged to see the original Cold Deck at Van Buren, Arkansas. Coke decided that if he could raise horses having the ability and intelligence of the Cold Decks, combined with some added style and refinement, he would have his ideal. Cold Deck's owner at that time was Foss Barker, who claimed his horse was the fastest animal on the globe. Coke reckoned he might have been, because people had just about given up trying to prove otherwise. Over the door to the horse's stall, wherever it might be, was hung a large sign reading, "Cold Deck Against the World!" So many people were ready to put money on Cold Deck that they would run him for a "nip of corn" or $10,000.

Cold Deck was born in 1862; he stood a scant 15 hands and was a dark sorrel. Foaled at Carthage, Missouri, Cold Deck was supposed to be a son of Steel Dust. Foss Barker told Coke that Cold Deck was sired by Steel Dust and related the following story. One day while Steel Dust was racing, he was left in the care of a groom while his owner went out of town. The groom immediately got into a poker game. One of the players had a mare which he wished to breed to Steel Dust, but Steel Dust's owner had given orders that his horse was not to be bred under any circumstances. Soon Steel Dust's groom had lost all of his money and had also promised to allow Steel Dust to be secretly bred. The colt that was later born bore the tell-tale name, Cold Deck. Whether this story is true or not is unknown, but who could pick a better sire for the great Cold Deck than Steel Dust?

The other story concerning the breeding of Cold Deck does not account for the name so neatly. According to this story, Tom Martin of Kyle, Texas, bred Cold Deck, his sire being Old Billy and his dam a quarter mare from Missouri. In either case the breeding is all of the same blood, so the question of which story is correct is academic.

The Cold Deck family, except in the Blake horses, has not been an independent line for many years. It has been mixed into the modern blood of the Joe Baileys, Rondos, Sykes, and Peter Mc-Cues. Some of Cold Deck's fastest get found their way into the *American Stud Book*, and many horses listed in the Appendix

32

claim Cold Deck as their sire. His blood was passed on through his sons Printer, Diamond Deck, Berry's Cold Deck, and Grey Cold Deck.

Ω Ω Ω Ω RONDO (1880) AND SYKES RONDO (1887)

Texas chalked up two more great Quarter Horse sires with the advent of the two Rondos. The original Rondo was Lock's Rondo, and when the name Rondo appears by itself, it is normally assumed that Lock's Rondo is the one in mind. Sykes Rondo should always have "Sykes" attached to avoid confusing him with the original. Rondo lived from 1880 until 1897 and Sykes Rondo from 1887 to 1907. Their sires were half brothers, both being by Old Billy.

Rondo was a chestnut son of the great Whalebone. Whalebone was by Old Billy by Shiloh and out of Mittie Stephens, who also was a granddaughter of Shiloh. Rondo was foaled in 1880 and was bred by Charles "Chick" Haley of Sweetwater, Texas. He stood about 15 hands and weighed 1,050 pounds. As a two-year-old he began racing and raced successfully for three years, when he was claimed under somewhat peculiar circumstances and taken to Kyle, Texas. In the spring of 1887, W. W. Lock was looking for a stallion to breed speed, and he purchased Rondo from Tom Martin for $1,000. This was a lot of money in those days. It was during that time that Lock owned Rondo that the Rondo family of short-horses was established. Rondo stood on Lock's ranch in Hays County until 1895, when Lock took him to Greer County, Oklahoma, where he died in 1897.[13]

Perhaps two of the best-known colts of Rondo were Little Rondo—also known as the Bunton Horse—and Blue Jacket. Blue Jacket beat Little Joe in a Mexican race, a feat that up until that time was considered impossible. This Little Joe was a gelding sired

13 I am indebted to Helen Michaelis for much of the information on Rondo. Some pertinent items were also obtained from O. W. Cardwell, one of the most interesting of West Texas Quarter Horse breeders and the last owner of Little Joe. After I had been out to Junction visiting Cardwell and his neighbor, J. D. Cowsert, I received a letter from Cardwell, dated January 7, 1940, saying "Texas Quarter Horses were all started by a sorrel, with a flax mane and tail, called Rondo, who was owned, bred, and buried by the Sykes family down in Karnes County." Three other men to whom I talked about Rondo were George Clegg, Will Copeland, and Frank Rook. *Denhardt Files*, Rondo Folders.

33

by Sykes Rondo and out of May Mangum. Blue Jacket became the short-horse ideal of Mexico, and his mounted likeness even appeared in Sanborn's in Mexico City.[14]

Little Rondo, or the Bunton Horse, gained fame on the short tracks and because of his son Yellow Jacket. Yellow Jacket, a dun horse foaled about 1908, was bred by Jim Barbee of Kyle, Texas, and was sold to W. T. Waggoner of Fort Worth.

The story of Sykes Rondo is somewhat similar. The Sykes string of horses was established by Crawford Sykes and Joe Mangum of Nixon, Texas. Sykes Rondo was a chestnut with a flax mane and tail and stood about 15–1 hands. He was by McCoy Billy by Old Billy by Shiloh and out of Grasshopper. He made his greatest contribution to the Quarter Horse world when crossed on the great mare, May Mangum. Old May was quite a mare, perhaps as great a producer as any Quarter Horse mare that ever lived. According to Ott Adams and George Clegg, she was of Tiger blood. From Sykes Rondo and Old May Mangum were raised Jenny, Little Joe (the gelding that went to Mexico), Baby Ruth, Nettie Harrison, Kitty, and Blue Eyes.

Jenny was the dam of Little Joe the stallion and King (Possum), and Traveler was their sire. Jenny also foaled Black Bess who became the dam of Cotton Eyed Joe. Baby Ruth was the dam of Paul El.

---

[14] *Official Stud Book and Registry of the American Quarter Horse Association,* I, 2, 19. Helen Michaelis wrote as follows: "Of Rondo's get, Blue Jacket and Little Rondo were the most famous. Blue Jacket was taken to Mexico to run against Little Joe. He beat him 60 feet of daylight on a pull, so the story goes, and could run a quarter in 21 seconds flat. Blue Jacket was so well known and so well loved in Mexico that his mounted likeness graced the halls of Sanbourn's, at that time the Jockey Club of Mexico, in Mexico City."

4. FOUNDATION HORSES

THE HORSES in this chapter, together with those found in the one before and the one following, have been somewhat arbitrarily selected and arranged. No book could include all the influential horses and mares, nor would it be desirable. For this reason I have attempted to satisfy only myself. Steel Dust is without doubt a "legendary hero," but separating Rondo and Traveler is harder to justify. The same could be said for Old Joe Bailey and Joe Reed. Date of foaling and date of death were useful guides in arranging these chapters.

Ω Ω Ω Ω DAN TUCKER (1887)

The Little Grove Stock Farm located near Petersburg, Illinois, was the home of many fast horses, but none brought it more fame than Dan Tucker. This speaks well for the efforts of Samuel Watkins, and Dan Tucker for that matter, as the Little Grove Stock Farm was also the home of Jack Traveler, Hi Henry, Peter McCue, Harmon Baker, Hickory Bill, Carrie Nation, and other well-known short-horses.[1]

One day when Watkins was traveling on business, he passed through Greene County, Illinois, where he saw the good mare June

---

[1] The most complete research made on the Watkins family was made by Bill Welsh, who left his business in East St. Louis to spend the time necessary to run down and talk to the surviving members and descendants of the Watkins family. He wrote up the results in his article, "Peter McCue's Family Tree," *The Quarter Horse Journal*, February, 1949. The first article on Peter McCue was Robert Denhardt's "Peter McCue, A Wonder Horse," *Cattleman*, October 1939. Two other pertinent articles on the Watkinses and their horses are "Dan Tucker," by Helen Michaelis, *Western Livestock Journal*, May, 1942, and "Dan Tucker in Illinois," by J. M. Huffington, *Quarter Horse*, July, 1949.

Bug. She was a half sister of Steel Dust, sired by Harry Bluff. June Bug's dam was Munch Meg by Snow Ball out of Monkey. Watkins was interested when he found out how she was bred, since he wanted to obtain some concentrated Steel Dust blood to infuse into his short-horses. He already had a son of Steel Dust named Jack Traveler. He felt that June Bug crossed by Jack Traveler would give him enough Steel Dust blood to produce some great horses. He could not have been more right.

Watkins was able to buy the mare and the following spring a little sorrel filly was born to June Bug so dainty and feminine that they called her Lady Bug. However, she did not mature this way. As she grew, her hindquarters became extremely large, and she was somewhat sway-backed. Her odd looks seemed no handicap because it was not long before she was running a hole in the wind. She got her name changed because of an accident. One day when she was being backed into a homemade starting chute, she ripped a gash in her rear quarters, but she won the race. From then on she was known as Butt Cut. Butt Cut was one of the fastest horses ever raised by the Little Grove Stock Farm. Nobody around Petersburg ever remembered her losing a race. Russ Watkins, a cousin, used to ride for Sam Watkins. Until he was about twenty and grew too heavy, he was a top-notch jockey. He rode many of the best Watkins horses, including Barney Owens, Dan Tucker, and Peter McCue. He says Butt Cut had more blinding speed than any horse he ever worked with.

When it became time to retire and breed Butt Cut, Sam Watkins took his prize mare up to New Berlin to breed her to the great stallion, Barney Owens. Barney was by Cold Deck by Billy Boy by Shiloh and out of a Steel Dust mare. On April 20, 1887, Butt Cut foaled a dark brown horse colt. Sam Watkins named him after a folk song his children were always singing called "Dan Tucker." Dan Tucker grew into a big horse, standing well over 15 hands and weighing in the neighborhood of 1,300 pounds. He began running as a two-year-old. His early races were match races in and around Manard County, Illinois. In 1890, he moved to the big tracks. *Goodwins Turf Guide* shows him entered in races at Spring-

36

field and St. Louis.[2] In 1892, he started eleven times, was in the money six times, and won once. His best time was in the half mile, where he won in forty-seven seconds.

Dan Tucker had many match races, but his most famous race was against his half brother, a horse named Sheriff. Fred T. Woods of Abilene, Texas, had gone up to Illinois and purchased a Barney Owens colt that he named "The Sheriff." The Sheriff had just about cleaned out North Texas and Kansas and had recently been running in Missouri and Illinois, looking for fresh money. Watkins was willing to race Dan Tucker, so a match was soon arranged. St. Louis was picked as neutral ground, and the horses were to run 440 yards, the best distance for both. The twenty-two seconds it took Dan Tucker to beat The Sheriff was the best officially recorded time run in Missouri up to that time, and perhaps since.

When Dan Tucker could no longer run, Watkins retired him to the stud. He was given a comfortable stall and corral for exercise near the stallion barn. Special care was given him as he had periodic ophthalmia or "moon blindness." One day a Thoroughbred stallion, The Duke of Highlands, got into Dan Tucker's corral and immediately attacked him. In his frantic efforts to avoid the other stallion, Dan Tucker ran into the large basswood tree in the corral. He dropped as if he had been shot. By the time he recovered consciousness, The Duke had been driven out of his corral and back into his own paddock, and the gate was wired shut. Dan Tucker, aside from a few cuts and bruises, seemed none the worse for the experience. It was a preview of things to come.

The fame of the Watkins horses spread throughout the shorthorse world. It became increasingly difficult for Watkins to keep his good horses. People in Texas were especially acquisitive. William Anson got Harmon Baker; George Clegg bought Hickory Bill; John Wilkins acquired Peter McCue; Tom Trammel, Dan Tucker and Caddie Griffith; Walter Handcock, John Wilkins; and

---

2 During the last half of the nineteenth century there were several periodicals devoted to turf statistics. *Bruce's Turf Register* began in 1870 and appeared each year until 1876, then it was taken over by *Turf Field and Farm*. *Goodwins Turf Guide* was published from 1883 until 1908 and contains the names and times of many famous Quarter Horses.

there were many others who obtained Watkins blood one way or another.

Trammel and Newman of Sweetwater, Texas, bought Dan Tucker in 1898. For the next fourteen years he had a happy home. Then one dark night another stallion got into his corral. This time, being old and stiff, he was unable to protect himself, and he was killed. Thus died Dan Tucker over fifty years ago. He was one of the greatest descendants of Steel Dust, and the progenitor of one of the best, if not the best, families of Quarter Horses.

Among the horses he sired are Barney Lee, Log Cabin, Tommy Tucker, Pat Tucker, Hi Henry, Hattie Shipley, Dolly Tucker, Harry N, Peter McCue, John Boone, Briggs, Hazel Hughlett, Katie Waddle, and Nona P. Some are worth saying a little more about to show the quality of Dan Tucker's progeny.

Hi Henry was inbred, as his dam, Butt Cut, was also Dan Tucker's dam. According to Helen Michaelis' records, Hi Henry was raced in 1896 by the New City Stables.[3] In 1893, he won five out of twelve starts. That year his best times were forty-eight seconds in the half-mile and fifty-nine for the four and one-half furlongs. In 1894, he won twelve out of thirty-one starts and was in the money in all but five. His best times were in the shorter distances, although he did run six furlongs in one minute, thirteen and one-fourth seconds, carrying 130 pounds. In this race he was ridden by one of the best jockeys of that day, Snapper Garrison. Once Snapper held track records in four different states simultaneously.

Nona P was one of the greatest brood mares sired by Dan Tucker. She was the dam of Harmon Baker, Bill Anson's famous shorthorse, and Buck Thomas. Both appear in many modern Quarter Horse pedigrees.

Dan Tucker could not be left out of any list of foundation animals.

Ω Ω Ω Ω OLD FRED (1893)

Two horses, Traveler and Old Fred, have hazy, or perhaps unknown, backgrounds. Coke Roberds told me that he did not know

3 Robert Moorman Denhardt, *The Quarter Horse*, II, 111.

Old Fred's breeding. However, other individuals who have been concentrating on the blood of Old Fred made prolonged investigations and believe that he came from Missouri and was by Black Ball.

It is fairly certain that old Fred was born in or very near the year 1893. He died in 1915. If he was bred as the investigations showed, he was by Black Ball, who was by Missouri Rondo and out of a mare by John Crowder, who was by Old Billy. This would make Old Fred a Steel Dust and Shiloh cross.

Those who have had the chance to use the blood of Old Fred, such as the Peavys, Semotans, Wiescamps, and Casements, are all enthusiastic about him. If Old Fred could be criticized, it would be because he was a little larger than the ordinary Quarter Horse and because he carried a good deal of white marking. However, his offspring left little to be desired in either conformation or speed. According to Coke, you could breed him to a boxcar and get a race horse.

Mrs. Evelyn P. Semotan,[4] outstanding Quarter Horse breeder, became interested in tracing the pedigree of Old Fred. She came by this interest naturally as she grew up in Quarter Horse country and was related to, or knew personally, all of the best Colorado Quarter Horse breeders. When she heard that Mark Choat came from Missouri (as Old Fred was rumored to have come) and was a lifetime devotee of short-horses, she wrote and asked him to come by and see her horses and talk Quarter Horse with her. The following is what he told Evelyn about Old Fred when he made his visit.

Old Fred, according to Choat, was foaled in 1894 at Lockwood, Missouri. He was out of a big palomino mare and by Black Ball. About 1900, Fred was owned by Jim Freeman of Lockwood. He took Old Fred and a full sister to Pueblo, Colorado. Later, in a trade, Bud Laughlin of Yampa, Colorado, got him. Bud used Old

---

[4] Evelyn Semotan, of Clark, Colorado, wrote about Old Fred and Coke Roberds. See "Old Fred, A Famous Stud," *The Quarter Horse Journal*, December, 1955. See also Cecil Hellbusch's "Coke T. Roberds," *The Quarter Horse Journal*, July, 1958. I met and talked with Coke Roberds on his Routt County ranch in Colorado in the 1930's and during the twenty-some years of our acquaintance we talked Quarter Horses countless times.

39

Fred as a freight horse, hauling supplies into northwestern Colorado.

The man who bought Old Fred from Laughlin and bred him so successfully was Coke Roberds. Roberds had a cow outfit at Hayden, Colorado, and like so many other cattlemen, he raised short-horses as a hobby. He had as fine a bunch of Steel Dust mares as there was in Colorado. The railway ended at that time at Walcott, and one day when Mr. and Mrs. Roberds were riding to Walcott on business, they met a freight outfit on the road. The wheel horse was Old Fred. Coke pulled up, stopped the freighter, and bought the yellow horse on the spot. Here again we have, as in the case of Traveler, a stallion working where you would logically expect to find a gelding. However, again like Traveler, this fact is not disputed. A few years after buying Old Fred, Roberds obtained Peter McCue. The cross of Peter McCue on Old Fred fillies produced many of the best Quarter Horses Colorado has seen.

Some of Old Fred's descendants are worth a word or two. There was Shiek, owned by the Peavys and the Matadors; there was Mary McCue, the dam of Ding Bob, Buck Thomas, and Squaw. Fred also sired Bob H, who still holds the Hayden track record for a quarter. Bob H also sired Papoose, a fast mare, and Papoose was the dam of Margie when bred to Ding Bob. When Papoose had some age on her, Marshall Peavy gave her to Jack Casement. For Jack she produced Cherokee Maiden when bred to Red Dog. Brown Dick, Plaudit, Old Nick, Question Mark, and many other famous Quarter Horses trace back to Old Fred.

Old Fred's death was premature. Mr. Roberds sold him to the Watson brothers of Burns Hole Country. He had lived there three years, when one day in the summer of 1915, the men, being in a hurry to get to town, threw him a bale of alfalfa without looking at it carefully. It was green. When they returned, Old Fred was dead.

Ω Ω Ω Ω PETER McCUE (1895)

Dan Tucker sired many great horses, but without doubt the greatest was Peter McCue. Peter McCue's blood had greater influence on the development of the Quarter Horse between 1900 and 1940 than that of any other single individual. His sons were in demand and scattered among all of the principal Quarter Horse areas. For example, Hickory Bill in South Texas, Harmon Baker in Central Texas, and John Wilkins in North Texas. The same was true in other states like Colorado, New Mexico, and Oklahoma, where sons of his were found out-running, out-performing, and out-producing all rivals.

Peter McCue's breeding explains his phenomenal success and tremendous ability. He was by Dan Tucker, whose story was told earlier in this book. Dan Tucker was a Shiloh and Steel Dust cross. Peter stood 16 hands high and weighed 1,430 pounds. He and Joe Hancock, his grandson, and Old Fred are the largest Quarter Horses to influence the breed significantly.

The first fame came to Peter McCue on the race track. He was principally a sprinter, running most of his races in Texas, Oklahoma, and Illinois.[5] While in Texas he spent much of his time in the vicinity of San Antonio. Those who knew him best claim that despite his size he was the fastest horse ever to run a short race. He ran what could be one of the fastest quarter miles ever run by a horse and recorded by more than one witness with a watch in hand. Three independent railbirds clocked him in twenty-one seconds flat. Since it was five o'clock in the morning and just a workout, it was not, of course, official. One other time he was supposed to have been clocked by several watches in the same time. Both of these could have been scored starts, although the modern records are getting closer to this time each season.

Peter McCue's speed was phenomenal, but he was a freak horse, as an examination of his pictures will show. Bob Wade ran a quarter in twenty-one and one-fourth seconds at Butte, Montana, and Rainbow by Senator, the horse of her day in Colorado, ran several races in around twenty-two seconds. Races run under twenty-two seconds are fairly common when some sort of a score or running start is used. Shue Fly ran an unofficial quarter at Albuquerque in twenty-one and two-tenths with a scored start. The

5 For a good account of Peter McCue see Wayne Dinsmore, "The Racing Record of Peter McCue," *The Quarter Horse Journal*, February, 1964, or "The Story of Peter McCue," *Quarter Horse*, September, 1948, by J. M. Huffington.

41

present world's record is twenty-one and eight-tenths for a standing start quarter set in 1957. When the American Quarter Horse Association, known as the AQHA, first listed official track records in 1945, Shue Fly held the quarter-mile record with a time of twenty-two and six-tenths.[6]

Peter McCue, when in San Antonio, was owned by John Wilkins, who later sold him to Milo Burlingame, who took him to Oklahoma. Some years later he was purchased by Coke Roberds. Roberds then kept him and cared for him until Peter McCue died in 1923 at the age of twenty-eight.

Among the famous race horses sired by Peter McCue are Carrie Nation, who at one time held the world's record for the five-eighth of a mile, and Buck Thomas, who ran forty-nine races and won thirty-eight. Many of Peter McCue's sons were kept as sires.

He represents one of the most important modern strains, and his bloodline has been carried on through his many sons and daughters. Some of them were Harmon Baker, Sheik, John Wilkins, Buck Thomas, Harry D, Hickory Bill, Duck Hunter, Carrie Nation, Chief, Jack McCue, and Badger. Harmon Baker sired Sancho, Harmon Baker, Jr., Seal Skin, Dodger, Big Nigger, and Little Joe (New Mexico). John Wilkins sired Joe Hancock.

Hickory Bill sired Paul El, Little Hickory Bill, Sam Watkins, and the Old Sorrel. Carrie Nation was the dam of Billy Sunday. Sheik sired Nick. Buck Thomas sired Bill Thomas. Jack McCue sired Barney Owens, Miss Santa Fe, Nancy M, Warrior, and others. Badger sired Old Midnight. It has been the privilege of few modern Quarter Horse sires to exert the influence that Peter McCue did upon the modern "short-horse."

Ω Ω Ω Ω TRAVELER (1900?)

It is most unusual, although not without precedence, for an unknown sire to beget a strain of horses. One such was Justin Morgan; another, Old Fred. Traveler, could be listed as the third, for he is a sire who came out of nowhere to establish a strain of Texas

---

[6] Melville H. Haskell, *The Quarter Running Horse* [1945]. This is the yearbook and register of merit of the American Quarter Racing Association.

Quarter Horses. From the ignominious position of pulling a scraper on the Texas and Pacific Railway, he rose to become the great Quarter Horse sire of his generation.

Traveler's history has been traced back to Eastland County, Texas, where he was working on the railway. He was just a sorrel work horse in a large *remuda* owned by the contractor. It has never been adequately explained just how it happened that a stallion was allowed with the horses, but there is no disagreement on this part of the story.[7] Traveler was not a young horse when he left the railroad—his age has been estimated at between eight and ten. He had to be broken to the saddle, even though trace-chain marks showed on his side and collar marks on his shoulders. He had been worked plenty but not ridden. According to one old-timer, he pitched terrifically but showed great intelligence and soon quieted down.

There are several stories about how he happened to leave the railroad. One has a man named Self trading a mule for him and driving him home hitched to the wagon with the remaining mule. Soon he was racing. One of his first races was against a mare named Mayflower. Will Crutchfield rode Mayflower. Bob Berry tells in a single sentence how the race came out: "Crutchfield could not have thrown a rock off Mayflower and touched Traveler's dust."[8]

Still another story has John Cooper and Brown Seay, who owned a saloon in Granbury, Texas, buying Traveler. One day Cooper drove to San Angelo in a buggy with a mule team. He noticed Traveler working in the railway fill pulling a fresno and admired him. He stopped on the spot and traded one of his mules for Traveler. When he got back to Granbury, he called his partner out to see Traveler, and they went for a ride. When Seay tapped the mule with the buggy whip the horse stepped out. Then Seay remarked, "He sure is some traveler." According to this account, that is how he was named.

In all of the stories, Brown Seay owned Traveler for a time, and

---

[7] Traveler was for the most part a mystery horse. Well-known writers have offered contradictory stories concerning him. Those interested in Traveler would do well to read Lewis Nordyke, "Traveler Country," *The Quarter Horse Journal*, December, 1954, and Nelson C. Nye, *The Complete Book of the Quarter Horse*, 215–26.

[8] Nye, *ibid.*, 216.

while Seay owned him he ran one of his best races against Bob Wilson, the top Quarter Horse in Central Texas. When he beat Wilson, his fame was made. Everyone who saw him commented on his powerful rear end. In a letter to me George Clegg said that Traveler had "the shortest back and biggest butt"[9] he had ever seen on a saddle horse. He added that he was a speckled sorrel and bred colts with gray hairs in their tails. He also bred quite a few colts with glass eyes. He bred his last colt in 1911.

Curiously, if it had not been for two mares, Fanny Pace and Jenny, Traveler might not have been considered the great sire he was. With Fanny as a dam, he sired Judge Thomas, Judge Welch, and Buster Brown, who was also known as Jack Tolliver. Bred to Jenny, he produced Little Joe, King or Possum, and Black Bess. None of his other colts ever came near to equaling any of these six.

Little Joe sired Zantanon, Joe Moore, Cotton Eyed Joe, and many others. Zantanon sired Hankin's King, Chico, San Simeon, Sonny Kimball, and many more. Possum sired Guinea Pig, who sired Tony, and Red Cloud, who in turn sired Mark.

Other of Traveler's well-known get were El Rey, Booger Red, Old Crawford, Texas Chief, John Gardner, and Chulo Mundo.

Traveler passed through several hands after he left Brown Seay, who was interested in him primarily as a running horse. For a while he was used as a ranch stallion and bred mares on Chris Seale's ranch near Baird, Texas. Traveler left the San Angelo country about 1903, staying briefly at Comanche, Big Lake, and Sweetwater. From Sweetwater, he was taken to South Texas by Will and Dow Shely of Alfred. Truly, Traveler was an exceptional horse.

Ω Ω Ω Ω LITTLE JOE (1904)

Little Joe of Alice, Texas, is the only horse of this name that has proved himself great enough that everyone knows he is meant when the name is spoken. His sire was Traveler, his dam Jenny, his full brother King. Traveler never would have been so famous were it not for King and his younger brother Little Joe—especially Little Joe.

[9] Letter dated in Alice, Texas, on December 14, 1939. *Denhardt Files*, Clegg Folder.

Dow and Will Shely bought Traveler in 1903 and brought him to their ranch between Alice and Alfred, Texas. The next year George Clegg looked over the crop of colts. George bought one. He said that the colt, named Little Joe, was so little he could put him in a chicken coop, and his wife wondered if he had to pay money for him, he was so tiny. But the colt grew up to have the same short back and big britches carried by his sire. He was also fast, and George raced him at every opportunity for four or five years. His first race was against Carrie Nation in San Antonio, and when he beat her he was a marked horse.

Some years later Ott Adams bought Little Joe but never ran him. He wanted a proven race horse to breed to his fast mares. He bred Little Joe for a number of years and then sold him, not because he wanted to, but because he was broke and needed money and O. W. Cardwell, of Junction, was willing to pay for him. Little Joe died on the Cardwell ranch in 1929. In a letter to Helen Michaelis, Cardwell wrote, "Little Joe crippled himself in a chute in 1929 and I had to shoot him." There is more to the story, but the above is sufficient.[10] Some people still argue whether Rondo or Little Joe did the most for the South Texas Quarter Horse.

There was no doubt in Ott Adams' mind that Little Joe did more for the Quarter Horse than any other horse since the Civil War. His get and grandget are still some of the best in the business. George Clegg, who raised Little Joe, considered him the fastest Quarter Horse he had ever run and probably as fast as any that ever ran in Texas. That's taking in considerable territory. O. W. Cardwell, who was never known to be at a loss for words, wrote, "Openly by many and secretly by more, he is considered the greatest most ideal sire of this century. Men who have his blood do not wish to change, and outsiders are hunting for it."[11]

Many great horses are sons and daughters of Little Joe. Some of his get include Ada Jones, Plain Jane, Adalina, Nita Joe, Balmy Days, Joe Moore, Zantanon, Grano de Oro, Old Poco Bueno,

[10] Letter dated in Junction, Texas, on February 13, 1940. *Denhardt Files*, Little Joe Folder.
[11] Letter dated in Junction, Texas, on January 7, 1940. *Denhardt Files*, Cardwell Folder.

Pancho Villa, Dan, Rainbow, Clear Weather, the Northington Horse, Mamie Jay, Little Sister, Clementia Garcia, Jim Wells, Pat Neff, Cotton Eyed Joe, Lupete, Lady Love, Ace of Hearts, and Dutch.

The names of his grandget are equally famous and include Miss Panama, Skidoo, Miss South Saint Mary's, Hill Country, Stella Moore, Hobo, Red Joe, Sunny Jim, King, and Billy Van. His great-grandget include Squaw H, Hank H, Clementine, Joe Barrett, Bo El, Bolo, Big Chief, Jesse, and countless others.

Joe Moore was one of Little Joe's most famous sons—not because he was a race horse nor because his head was so stylish, but because he produced so many horses that could run, rope, cut, and win shows.

In another section of this book, the story of Della Moore is told. She was the dam of Joe Moore. Ott Adams bought her just to breed to Little Joe in order to have a suitable replacement. He bred Della to Little Joe the day she arrived on the ranch. The first foal she delivered was a filly. The next year she was dry. The following year she foaled Grano de Oro, a fine bay stallion. Ott still did not have the stud colt he wanted. Della's next and last colt was Joe Moore. He was foaled on March 23, 1927. Ott took one look at the foal and was happy.

Joe Moore grew up into a splendid bay stallion so typically a Quarter Horse that no one would ever mistake his breed, even if he were drawn down and ready to race. He was, in the usual manner of the early Quarter Horses, a small horse when height was considered. He always looked big but measured small. Some horses may be like some men. Take Napoleon, for instance. Nobody ever thought of him as being little, but he was. Perhaps it was the same with Joe Moore. When you walked up to chin him, you found his withers were just 14–2 hands. He was, outside of his head, which was a typical South Texas head, perfectly proportioned for a Quarter Horse. He had good hips, hind legs, shoulders, middle, forelegs —everything one could wish.

All of Joe Moore's life was spent in siring foals, such as Bumps, Hobo, Adam, Kitty Wells, Buddy Lewis, Lucky Boots, Payday, V

Day, Jo-mo-ca, Joe Etta, Stella Moore, Monita, Lee Moore, Joe Less, Poquita Mas, and others too numerous to mention.

Once Ott sold Joe Moore to J. Rogers of Menard, Texas. This was the only time the two were separated, and Ott spent sleepless nights until he was able to rescind the sale and bring him home. Joe Moore certainly was one of the best, if not the best, of Little Joe's colts. When Joe Moore died, Ott buried him near Little Joe, whose bones he had brought back from Junction and buried on his farm. Today, all three, Little Joe, Ott Adams, and Joe Moore sleep under the same Texas soil—three individuals to whom the Quarter Horse owes much.

Ω Ω Ω Ω KING OR POSSUM (1905)

Many famous Quarter Horses had several names. One of these was King, who was also called Possum or King Cardwell. King had one distinction, that of siring well-known horses in Texas and then going to Arizona and, under the name of Possum, starting a whole new strain of Quarter Horses. King was not just another horse; he was a full brother of Little Joe, sired by Traveler and out of the famous Jenny by Sykes Rondo. Traveler was undoubtedly a great sire, but take away the offspring of the fabulous Jenny and his stature diminishes. Some experts consider King the greatest colt sired by Traveler.

King's story begins a little over sixty years ago, down in South Texas near the little town of Alice. Here a sorrel horse colt was foaled by one of the greatest Quarter mares of all times—Jenny, by Sykes Rondo by McCoy Billy by Old Billy by Shiloh. Jenny was out of May Mangum, a descendant of Tiger. The breeder, Dow Shely, looked the little fellow over and predicted that he would be king of all he surveyed some day, so "King" he became. This was in 1905. He became a King, even though he was known most of his life as Possum. He died in 1925, respected and admired by horsemen in half a dozen different states. He grew up to be a light sorrel with considerable roan hairs, so light in his flanks and legs as to be almost dun colored.

Old Jenny did not live to suckle King; she was old and worn out,

47

and King was her last effort. King was raised by hand by Dick Herring, who bought him and raised him as a dogie. He grew up strong and sturdy and fleet as the wind.

King was never noted as a race horse. Ed Echols saw him in most of his better-known races, and he felt he could run as fast as was necessary. He remembered King's match with Yellow Jacket. He saw several watches afterwards and said that if the clocks were accurate the time was amazing. This famous race, when King beat the champion Yellow Jacket, took place on the O. G. Park track near Kyle, Texas. King was reported to have won a race at San Antonio in twenty-one and one half seconds.

King was sold to J. J. Kennedy of Bonita, Arizona, who paid the fantastic price of one-hundred head of sound, young horses. Since Kennedy already had a horse named King, he renamed this one Possum. Possum was apparently never matched when he reached Arizona. On the way to Wilcox for a race he was led up to a leaking water trough, his left hind leg bogged down in the mud, and he pulled a leader when he strained to release his leg. His racing days were over.

A number of years ago, the founder of modern organized short racing, Melville H. Haskell, discovered some interesting facts about King, whom he called Possum, his Arizona name. Haskell was compiling records in 1944 for his annual booklet of short-racing statistics for the American Quarter Racing Association. Of the approximately two hundred horses that had run between 1941 and 1944 on tracks approved by the AQRA, only thirty-nine had shown sufficient ability to be classed as Celebrated American Quarter Running Horses, the highest honor given the running horses. Of this thirty-nine, thirty-one traced directly through the male line to seven families. All of these seven families were Thoroughbred except one, Traveler. The Traveler line, headed by his son King or Possum, was the outstanding single producer, accounting for nine, or almost one-fourth of the entire list of Celebrated horses.[12]

---

[12] Haskell, *Racing Quarter Horses 1944*, 13. Haskell, who worked closely with all of the short-horses running in the early 1940's was so successful that Tucson bec me

Most folks in Texas would say that King's greatest son was Joe Bailey of Gonzales. More about him appears in the following chapter, although it might be of interest to note here that Joe Bailey's son, Little Joe, Jr., was taken to Arizona and his offspring today are competing with other descendants of King.

It is difficult to pick out the best of King's Arizona get. Some horsemen would probably select Red Cloud and Guinea Pig, although Blue Eyes was an outstanding horse. Some of the better-known race horses tracing to Red Cloud were Jeep B, Red Racer, Pay Dirt, and Pay Toll. Guinea Pig was the grandsire of Buster, Tonta Gal, and Chester C. Blue Eyes was the grandsire of Prissy. The dam of Clabber was a granddaughter of King. One of the greatest sires of cow horses and rodeo horses was Mark, who was sired by Red Cloud.

King was quite a horse, even when he was Possum.

Ω Ω Ω Ω JOE BAILEY (1907)

Joe Bailey of Weatherford, the first and most important Joe Bailey, was bred by Dick Baker of Weatherford, Texas. He was foaled in 1907 when a local politician named Joe Bailey was campaigning, during the height of an oil scandal, for the Senate on the national Democratic ticket. Needless to say, Dick Baker was a good Democrat and strong supporter of Senator Bailey, who won the election. No one was especially surprised when the little sorrel stud colt was named for Baker's favorite senator, Joe Bailey.

Most great horses are the product of two outstanding bloodlines. Joe Bailey was a cross by Steel Dust and Shiloh. He was sired by Eureka and out of Susie McQuirter. Eureka was by Shelby by Tom Driver of Steel Dust. Tom Driver's dam was Mammoth by Shiloh. Shelby's dam was Mittie Stephens, who was a granddaughter of Shiloh. Eureka was out of Jenny Capps, whose dam was Mounts

the Quarter Horse racing capital of the world and nobody contested the right to hold there each year a World's Championship quarter-mile race. The fastest horses in the United States came to compete—Clabber, Shue Fly, Barbra B, Miss Bank, Piggin String, Queenie, Miss Princess, Dee Dee, and others too numerous to mention. Haskell was probably the only person in the United States in a position to know where the best horses were coming from. For more information see "Organized Short Racing," Chapter 8.

49

by Steel Dust. Susie McQuirter was by Little Ben by Barney by Steel Dust. She was out of Aury by Dutchman by Rondo by Whalebone by Billy by Shiloh. Joe Bailey of Weatherford was royally bred.

Joe Bailey's sire, Eureka, was standing on Colonel Couch's ranch in Central Texas when, in 1906, Baker arrived at the ranch in a buckboard, with his good mare Susie McQuirter tied on behind. The following year a beautiful sorrel Quarter Horse stud colt dropped by Susie was named Joe Bailey. Although Joe Bailey lived until 1934, it could be said that he was born twenty years too soon. He spent the better part of thirty years in Central Texas, and you could count on your fingers the number of good Quarter Horse mares that went to his court.

In time Joe Bailey was sold to Bud Parker. Bud kept him for many years and then sold him to Jack Tindell of Eastland County. Later Jack sold him to E. A. Whiteside of Sipe Springs, Texas, who owned Joe Bailey until his death in June of 1934.

Most of Joe Bailey's sons were gelded and sold as ranch horses and his daughters were put into ranch *remudas*. Those sons who were not gelded, like Yellow Wolf, were owned by ranchers who bred for their own use, not for sale, so the blood was not scattered. Most of Joe Bailey's fillies were bred to remount stallions.

W. T. Waggoner's two stallions, Yellow Wolf and Yellow Bear, were by Joe Bailey of Weatherford and out of Old Mary.

One of Whiteside's mares, Maudy Bailey, produced Buckskin Joe when bred to Fred Bailey, a son of Joe Bailey. One race horse by Joe Bailey became fairly well known. His name was Jimmie Allred. He raced all over Texas and ended up in the hands of Helen Michaelis, who used him as a stud in her breeding program. Two fast fillies by Joe were Peggy Ray, owned by Pete Tindale, and Roan Peggy, owned by Coke Blalock. One of the few breeders to obtain several Joe Bailey mares was R. L. Underwood, who had Rita Fidler, Georgia Lee, and Josie Bailey. Frank Austin also had some good Bailey mares like Grey Peggy. Perhaps the top rodeo horse to be sired by Joe Bailey was Stranger, the great bulldogging horse owned by Mike Hastings.

COLONIAL RACE HORSE
Typical Celebrated American Quarter Running Horse. Such was the foundation stock of the modern day Quarter Horse.

THE

AMERICAN STUD BOOK:

CONTAINING FULL PEDIGREES OF ALL THE IMPORTED

THOROUGH-BRED STALLIONS AND MARES,

WITH THEIR PRODUCE, INCLUDING THE

ARABS, BARBS, AND SPANISH HORSES,

FROM THE

EARLIEST ACCOUNTS OF RACING IN AMERICA, TO THE END OF THE YEAR
1872; ALSO, ALL THE NATIVE MARES AND THEIR PRODUCE.

ALPHABETICALLY ARRANGED.

WITH AN APPENDIX,

*GIVING PEDIGREES OF ALL THE NATIVE STALLIONS WHOSE DAMS HAVE
NO NAMES, WITH FULL AND COPIOUS INDEX TO
PRODUCE OF THE MARES.*

BY

S. D. BRUCE,

Editor of the "Turf, Field and Farm."

L. C. BRUCE, CO-EDITOR.

IN TWO VOLUMES.—VOL. I.

A to L.

REVISED IN 1884. WITH SUPPLEMENTARY INDEX.

NEW YORK:

SANDERS D. BRUCE

"TURF, FIELD AND FARM."

TITLE PAGE FROM BRUCE'S AMERICAN STUD BOOK
Containing names of many early Quarter Horses.

Pedigree  of

Dan Tucker,

The famous racing-stallion now owned and kept by Thos. Trammell, Sweetwater, Texas.

Dan Tucker was sired by Barney Owens. 1st dam, Butt Cut, by Jack Traveller, he by Steel Dust, out of Queen, who was sired by Pilgrim, by Lexington. 2nd dam, June Bug, by Harry Bluff the sire of Steel Dust. 3rd Dam, Munch Meg, by Snow Ball. 4th Dam, Monkey, by Boanerges.

Jack Traveller was sired by old Steel Dust. Dam, Queen, by Pilgrim, by Lexington. Harry Bluff is Whip and Timoleon stock, and was sired by Short Whip, out of Big Nance, a thoroughbred mare. Barney Owens was sired by Cold Deck, and out of the Overton mare. Cold Deck was by Billy Boy, he by Shiloh, and out of a Steel Dust mare. Cold Deck's dam was Dolly Coker, by Old Rondo.

For further information in regard to this famous breed of racers, address.

Thos. Trammell,   Sweetwater, Texas,

STALLION-AT-STUD ADVERTISEMENT
Showing Dan Tucker's pedigree.

SIR ARCHY
Probably second only to Old Janus, to whom the
Quarter Horse owes much.

FROM HERBERT'S *Frank Forester's Horse and Horsemanship*

PETER McCUE
Forefather of many of the outstanding Quarter Horses.
His lineage traces to Steel Dust.

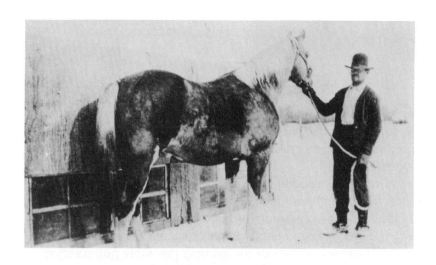

OLD FRED (*above*)
A Steel Dust and Shiloh cross.

OLD JOE BAILEY OF WEATHERFORD
A great sire of North Texas—pictured in his old age.

TRAVELER, THE MYSTERY HORSE (*above*)
Sire of Little Joe, King (Possum), and Texas Chief.

COURTESY NELSON NYE

LITTLE JOE
Ott Adams' stud that started a new family of Quarter
Horses in South Texas.

K<small>ING</small> (P<small>OSSUM</small>) (*above*)
Cross of Traveler and Jenny by Sykes Rondo.

D<small>ELLA</small> M<small>OORE</small>
Grande Dame of the Quarter Horse world.

In some respects the most famous producing filly of Joe Bailey was the one that was out of the Nixon mare by Billie Dribble by Anthony by Old Billy. She dropped a sorrel horse colt that was named after his grandfather, Joe Bailey, and is generally referred to as Joe Bailey of Gonzales. He is discussed in detail later. Considering how few of his offspring are known, it is a wonder Joe Bailey of Weatherford ever achieved the fame he did.

Ω Ω Ω Ω YELLOW JACKET (1907)

Charles Haley of Sweetwater, Texas, bred and raised Rondo, as has been related. Our interest in Rondo here begins after he was purchased by W. W. Lock, who wanted him for breeding purposes.

Jim Barbee of Kyle, Texas, had an outstanding yellow mare purchased from Albert Leath of Hay County. Her dam had come from Mexico, and Leath liked the dam so well that he took her to the best stallion he knew, Lock's Rondo. He wanted a horse colt. When a filly was foaled, he sold it to Jim Barbee. This filly was destined to become the dam of Yellow Jacket when bred to Little Rondo, her half brother.

All the Rondos could run; and Yellow Jacket early showed such speed that by the time he was a two-year-old he was on the quarter-mile circuit. He was raced for five or six years and then was purchased by W. T. Waggoner, who was always trying to buy and raise more and faster horses than his neighbors, the Burnetts. Waggoner immediately began to breed Yellow Jacket. According to Lige Reed, this was in 1916. Lige describes Yellow Jacket as being a dun with a red mane and tail, around 15 hands high. He was well formed, compact, and had an excellent disposition. While in the ownership of the Waggoners, Yellow Jacket sired Beetch's Yellow Jacket, Yellow Ding Bob, and East's Yellow Jacket.

When the Waggoners had all of the Yellow Jacket mares that they needed, the old horse was given to Lee Bivens of Amarillo. When Yellow Jacket was nineteen, Bivens bred him to five mares belonging to Edgar Thompson. The next spring the old horse's ability was again proved when four horse colts and a filly were foaled. Among these were Blackburn, Yellow Boy, and Cowboy.

51

Cowboy hit the jackpot a few years later when he began siring colts of the caliber of Hardtwist and Shue Fly. Yellow Boy was sold to the JA's, where he stood for many years siring top cow horses. He was later sold to John Sims of Pampa, who in turn sold him to Ralph Jones of Claude. Blackburn was purchased by the Waggoner Three D ranch and became one of its most successful sires, living out his life on the Waggoner estate.

Probably the high point of Yellow Jacket's career (outside the stud) was his famous race with King. King was the son of Traveler that went to Arizona and became known as Possum. King lived almost a hundred miles south and west of Yellow Jacket. He was the big gun of the short tracks from San Antonio to Nuevo Laredo and from Brownsville to San Angelo. Yellow Jacket was equally well known in his home area, which was roughly the triangle formed by Austin, Beeville, and Houston.

Yellow Jacket against King was a natural. It was only a question of when and where. Both had run better than two lengths of daylight ahead of all other competition. They belonged to the so-called open to the world class. It must be remembered that "open to the world" meant if agreement on the details, such as where, when, judges, weights, forfeit money, and so on, could be reached. Some little time went by after the original contact before all the conditions were acceptable to both sides. In order for final arrangements to be made, it was necessary to build a new track so that neither horse would have the advantage of a "home" track. In 1911 the race was matched. Each side was so sure of the superiority of its horse that to get money down was easy. When the trainload of supporters of King returned home to Devine, they were a happy and prosperous group. That was the day and the race that broke the town of Kyle, Texas.

The Quarter Horse Journal carried the following story by Franklin Reynolds. He obtained it from Tom Garrett, who trained King for this race and in whom King's owner, Dick Herring, had the utmost confidence.

I never had seen Yellow Jacket but his reputation had me greatly interested. Just as soon as we reached Kyle, Mr. Herring got me to go and look at him before too many more bets were made. As soon as I saw Yellow Jacket I felt confident Little King could win the race. Yellow Jacket's back was too long and he was standing with his feet out behind him, and not collected under him. I went back and told Mr. Herring that Yellow Jacket wouldn't be able to get even close to our horse. I understand we broke the bank at Kyle that day, that they ran clear out of money. We must have won at least twenty thousand dollars on that race. I had galloped King quite a bit and several times had carried him the quarter in twenty-one seconds with a running start. I didn't see how we could lose. Yellow Jacket didn't look to me like a horse who could beat him, and sure enough he couldn't.[13]

In the race, King pulled out ahead in the first 250 yards, but when they reached the 300-yard marker, Yellow Jacket made his play. At first it appeared that he could take King, as he pulled up even with King's jockey, but from somewhere the Traveler colt summoned the little extra that all champions have and was able to hold off the determined bid by Yellow Jacket. King won by scant head. There have been great races down through the years— Twigg and Paddy Whack, Steel Dust and Shiloh, Dan Tucker and Sheriff, and Clabber and Shue Fly—but it is doubtful that two greater horses than King and Yellow Jacket, both of whom were to establish outstanding families, ever met in a tighter or more thrilling race.

Cowboy was one of the better-known sons of Yellow Jacket. He was bred by Ed Thompson and foaled in 1927. His dam was Roan Lady by Stalks by John Wilkins by Peter McCue and his second dam was Bonnie Wilkins by John Wilkins.[14] Cowboy was sometimes called Cowpuncher. He was the sire of two of the best Quarter running horses when short racing returned to favor in the forties—Shue Fly and Hardtwist.

Another well-known son of Yellow Jacket was Beetch's Yellow Jacket, who was foaled in 1922. He was born on the Three D at

---

13 "Yellow Jacket, a Most Wonderful Horse," *The Quarter Horse Journal*, June, 1959, 18.

14 The pedigree here is from an old sheet of paper given Roy Hepler by Ed Thompson. *Denhardt Files*, Yellow Jacket Folder.

Electra and could be easily recognized as a Waggoner colt by the D branded on his shoulder. He was purchased from the ranch by Mike Beetch in 1924.

While everyone is satisfied that Beetch's Yellow Jacket was sired by Yellow Jacket, there is some question about his dam. At first Beetch listed his Yellow Jacket as being out of a mare by Waggoner's Yellow Wolf. This would have made his dam a granddaughter of the Weatherford Joe Bailey. However, further checking with individuals who were working on the Waggoner ranch at that time, such as Lige Reed and Will Steed, indicates that Beetch's Yellow Jacket may have been a daughter or granddaughter of their earlier Yellow Wolf, who was sired by Pid Hart. This Yellow Wolf was bought by Waggoner from the Brown Brothers of Fort Worth; he had a formidable short racing record. When Yellow Jacket was first brought to the ranch, his first mares were mainly daughters of the Yellow Wolf from Fort Worth.

The first race Beetch's Yellow Jacket ran was at Lawton, Oklahoma, against a well-known local horse called George Washington. During the next five years he was beaten only once, and that was by Cowpuncher. Although it is hard to verify that Cowpuncher was Ed Thompson's horse (better known as Cowboy), it is almost certainly the case, and if this is the case, the only horse to beat him was his half brother.

Beetch's Yellow Jacket was a light dun with black mane and tail. He stood 15 hands and weighed 1,135 pounds in racing shape. Beetch sold Yellow Jacket to the Burnett ranch in 1930; Tom Burnett paid $500 for him—almost a record for those days. Some of his best-known progeny were Lady Coolidge, Dixie Beach (should have been Beetch), and a stallion that ended up on the JA Ranch known as the JA Yellow Jacket.

Yellow Jacket, thanks to the Mexican or Spanish blood in his mother, produced what is probably the outstanding line of dun Quarter Horses. He died on the Triangle Ranch.

Ω Ω Ω Ω DELLA MOORE (1912)

A stallion's opportunity for good or bad can appear on two or three

54

hundred colts during his lifetime. A mare, on the other hand, has only ten or fifteen chances to show her worth. Perhaps this is one of the reasons why this seems to be a male world most of the time. Nevertheless, ever so often a female will come along whose influence is so great that she cannot be ignored. Jenny, for example, was the dam of both Little Joe and King (Possum). Della Moore was the dam of Joe Moore, Joe Reed, and Grano de Oro. It is clear that Della Moore was not just an incubator. There is no other Quarter Horse, stallion or mare, who has as many descendants outstanding in every performance classification. A matriarch such as she can influence and has influenced the Quarter Horse world for many years.

One must travel to Louisiana to start the story. Here in the Cajun country horseflesh showing fleetness was a commodity well understood. Louisiana is in many ways the home of the modern short-horse if racing is the criterion. It produced more fast short-horses between 1900 and 1940 than any other single area in the country. Della Moore was born a few miles north of Scott, Louisiana, on a farm owned by Ludovic Stemmans. When the occasion offered itself, which it did with some regularity, Ludovic was happy to match a race with one or more of his horses. His favorite horse was Bell, a daughter of Sam Rock, who was a smooth sorrel mare of about 15 hands. However, she had taken the slack out of so many horses she was getting a little hard to match, so he decided to breed her. He was about to breed her to Dewey, the fastest horse around his area, when suddenly Dewey was matched 256 yards and lost. Therefore Bell ended up at the court of Dedier, the winner, and the resulting offspring Ludovic called Della Moore.

In the early 1900's, Della ran her first race when she was still suckling her mother. The Cajuns were never noted for patience, and Ludovic wanted to see his new filly run. So a "milk race" was arranged with one of his neighbors. These races were common then and served a dual purpose; they gave breeders a line on their prospects and at the same time gave them an opportunity to bet some money, furniture, wagons, or whatever else wasn't tied down. The colts were taken to the race track and then not allowed to

55

nurse their mothers for a while. They then were held at the starting chute by two men while the mothers were led nickering away, up the track, generally 156 yards. At the given signal the colts were turned loose, and away they sprinted looking for milk. Della Moore was the easy winner, and her feed and board were paid in advance. By the time she was in her second year, it became more and more difficult to match Della. She was too well known in the parishes around Lafayette. An agreement was made between Ludovic and a friend, Demonstran Broussard to race her farther from home. Broussard later transferred Della Moore to Boyd Simar, another race horse man who traveled all over the Southeast racing short-horses. Boyd lived a couple of parishes south, in Abbeville.

Boyd Simar's life was running horses; it had been his father's before him and was his son's, Paul's, after him. Boyd and Paul became well known in short-horse circles when they trained race horses for Jack Hutchins and Johnny Ferguson.[15] Both Boyd and Paul spoke Cajun French by preference and English only with an inimitable accent. Della lived up to Boyd's expectations, and he won a lot of money on her and lost most of it betting on his other horses.

Texas in those days had many "bull rings," small circular tracks, some only quarter of a mile around. If no "bull ring" was available, at least a straightaway path could be found. At most fairs and celebrations race meets were held, although parimutuels and organized betting were prohibited. Betting itself was common, and the sheriff was often the stakeholder. Top horses such as Della Moore could not get in the races (all the others would withdraw), but generally a local horseman could be talked into a match race if conditions were right. When Boyd could not match Della any more, he sold her to Henry Lindsay of Granger, Texas. Early in 1920 she was taken to a race meet at San Antonio and stabled next to the fine stallion Joe Blair, one of the fastest race horses alive.

---

[15] I managed the Hutchins and Ferguson Quarter Horses while Boyd and Paul Simar were training for them. It was directly from Boyd that I obtained most of my information about Della Moore and other Louisiana short-horses. Several times I made trips into Louisiana with, or after, race horses and so came to know many of the men connected with Dedier, Flying Bob, Della Moore, and other well-known Louisiana race horses.

His famous match race with Pan Zareta had taken place several years before, at Juárez, when he had established a new world's record of thirty-nine seconds for three and one-half furlongs. He was still in his prime. While Joe Blair and Della Moore were in San Antonio, stabled in adjoining stalls, the horse known as Joe Reed was conceived. Boyd Simar had no idea how or why Della was bred to Joe Blair, for she was racing at the time.

One day George Clegg told the owner of Little Joe, Ott Adams, about a Louisiana mare he had seen that could run even better than she looked, and she was a walking picture. They talked about Della Moore's breeding, and Ott decided she might be the one to give him a son to replace the aging Little Joe. Ott wanted to see Della Moore and at the same time look over her colt, Joe Reed. He did, and he then knew she was the mare he wanted. Her stature, her clean-cut limbs, and her femininity would cross well with Joe's compact masculinity. And with that breeding, speed on both sides, he felt the offspring should fly. The owner promised to call Ott when he was ready to sell.

Some time went by, and Ott Adams began to get restless. Little Joe would soon be twenty years old, and Ott still did not have Della to breed to him. He decided he wouldn't wait any longer. He drew some money out of the bank. He had to pay $600 for Della, a large sum of money in that day for an old mare that could no longer run. However, Ott figured time was running out on both Little Joe and Della Moore and there was no choice.

As soon as Della Moore arrived in Alice, Ott bred her to Joe. Her first foal by Little Joe was dropped August 16, 1923, a beautiful little sorrel filly he named Aloe. John Dial came by to see Little Joe's and Della's first daughter and liked her so well he bought her on the spot. Ott bred Della back to Joe when Aloe was nine days old, but she did not stick. She came in regularly, but Joe could not seem to get her in foal. Ott was to learn later that she would foal only every other year regardless of whom she was bred to or how often.

In 1925, Della foaled Grano de Oro. For some reason, good as the colt was, he did not satisfy Ott, so when John Dial showed up,

57

Ott sold Della's second colt to him just as he did her first. She would not settle that year. On March 23, 1927, Della Moore foaled the bay horse colt sired by Little Joe that suited Ott, and so he gave the new colt his sire's first name and his dam's last, Joe Moore. Ott was satisfied with Joe Moore and sold Little Joe to O. C. Cardwell of Junction. Della Moore foaled one more filly before she died in 1930—the filly Panzarita by Paul El.

Thus ends the saga of Della Moore, a peerless race mare and the *grande dame* of the Quarter Horse world.

5. EARLY MODERN SIRES

F ROM THIS POINT ON, all the horses discussed lived in the twentieth century. I was fortunate enough to be acquainted with nearly all of these horses, and in every case knew the breeder or owner. Most of the information on them, therefore, is first hand.

Ω Ω Ω Ω CONCHO COLONEL (1904)

Dan Casement read with great interest an article appearing in the *Breeders' Gazette*. In it was pictured a sturdy but graceful stud horse, the caption saying he was of Quarter Horse breeding. Accompanying the photograph was a short story by the breeder of the stallion, William Anson, of Texas.[1] This was in 1910. Dan liked what he saw in the picture, and he began to correspond with the author to find out more about the breed. The eventual result was that Casement bought a Quarter Horse, Concho Colonel, from Anson. Concho Colonel was by Jim Ned and cost Casement $500. This was a lot of money for an unregistered horse of strange parentage—at least strange to Dan Casement. However, Dan always felt it was one of the greatest buys he ever made.

Dan Casement did not purchase the stallion immediately after getting in touch with Anson. He was, at the time, looking at some horses sired by The Senator, a Thoroughbred that was standing at Kiowa, Colorado. Eventually, he decided to buy the Quarter Horse, and Concho Colonel was shipped to Colorado Springs, where Casement was living at that time. Here is Dan Casement's own description of what the Colonel looked like when he arrived at Colorado Springs.

1 "Breeding a Rough Country Horse," *The Breeders' Gazette*, May, 1910.

59

He was a beautiful dappled chestnut, compactly built, smooth and well balanced in shape, with short back, deep barrel, and long belly. Most noticeable was his immense muscular development which seemed to reach a climax amounting almost to a positive deformity in his bulging jaws. Had he been human, I would have suspected a bad case of mumps. I subsequently learned that this appearance is characteristic of the Steel Dust strain. Indeed in some localities Quarter Horses are commonly called "Big Jaws."[2]

Concho Colonel was sent on to Unaweep Canyon where Casement had a ranch. Here he was to service the brood mare band, made up of eleven mares he had purchased from Charley Walker of Kiowa. Walker had owned two well-known Colorado short-horses, Little Steve and The Senator, and the mares were of this breeding. This account of Concho Colonel is in Dan Casement's words.

> For 16 years, until he died at the age of 23, Concho Colonel was a real institution on the Unaweep. He had all the priceless qualities, both of conformation and character, that mark the typical Bull-dog Quarter Horse. He knew all there was to know about cows and how to handle them. This wisdom and skill he consistently bequeathed to his progeny."[3]

Dan Casement was partial to one of his mares named Little Judge. She was by Little Steve out of Sal by Grey Joe. As time went by, Dan decided that she should be the one to furnish him a successor to replace the Colonel. In 1914 she dropped the colt that Dan had been waiting for. He named the colt Balleymooney and took him to his Kansas Juniata farm. Here he stayed for some sixteen years. Then Dan decided it was time for Balleymooney to return home, so he loaded him up and trailed him behind his Model A, nine hundred miles over the mountains to his birthplace in the Unaweep Canyon.

Dan and his son Jack, who by this time was running the Triangle Bar, carefully selected Balleymooney's mares. They were for

2 "Steel Dusts as I Have Known Them," *American Hereford Journal*, June, 1927, 245.

3 "From Punce to Deuce," *The American Hereford Journal*, July, 1954, 677.

the most part CS mares, bred by Ed Springer of Springer, New Mexico. The last crop foaled in 1933. Balleymooney died that winter.

Springer's Little Joe, the sire of Balleymooney's last mares, was a son of Anson's Harmon Baker, perhaps the best-known short-horse in Texas at the time. Harmon Baker was a son of Peter McCue. Purchased by Anson in 1908, he soon became famous in Texas as a sire of short-horses. Now back to Balleymooney, whose sire, Jim Ned, was also an Anson stallion.

When spring came to the Unaweep that year, the foals began to arrive. Five of Balleymooney's foals out of the CS mares were stallions and four were fillies. The five stallions, each of whom became famous in his own right, were Red Dog, Frosty, Deuce, Billy Byrne, and Buckshot. Balleymooney had done himself proud in his last year. A long, useful life had come to a fitting climax with a priceless crop of colts.

Since Dan Casement was spending his time on the Juniata farm in Kansas, it was Jack Casement's responsibility to look after the horses. In fact, it was Jack who made Triangle Bar horses famous throughout the Quarter Horse world. Jack picked Red Dog to keep as his top stallion. Dan selected the Deuce to take to Kansas to replace Balleymooney. Within a few years the other stallions left the ranch to establish reputations for themselves in other parts of the country.

Dan always felt that Deuce was a replica of his sire Balley-mooney, and he became Dan Casement's personal mount. In the true tradition of the old-time Quarter Horse breeder, Dan was a "stud-horse" man, always riding a stallion by choice. The disposition of most Quarter Horses not only made it possible but pleasurable. One further quite from Dan before we turn to to his son Jack Casement.

For nearly two score years three grand horses—three genera-tions of the same blood, Concho Colonel, Balleymooney, and the Deuce—shared my life most intimately. In work and in play they were my faithful friends. In my lighter hours they added greatly to

61

my gaiety and happiness; in times of trouble I turned to them for consolation.[4]

Red Dog and his brothers all grew up to be remarkable, dignified, and far-famed Quater Horse stallions. In conformation they typified the Steel Dust strain with all its strong points, and all of its so-called weak points that those partial to Thoroughbred blood like to criticize in the Quarter Horse. It is just those "bull-dog" features—the short ears, the bulging jaws, the short back, the heavily muscled rear quarters, the sloping croup with the low set tail, the abbreviated cannons and pasterns, and the heavy, broad shoulders and deep, deep heart with a long, long underline—that characterize the Quarter Horse and set him apart from the Thoroughbred.

Let's see what happened to Casement's crop of colts.

Red Dog had none of the qualities of the Thoroughbred. Like his sire and grandsire he was a Steel Dust Quarter Horse and could never have been mistaken for anything else, regardless of age or condition. His conformation proved his heritage. It was stamped on every line of his compact, athletic body.[5]

No one can really tell someone else about a horse as well as the owner and breeder. Following are Jack's words when describing Red Dog.

His one idea was to get all work over with as soon as possible. To this end he studied ways and means at his leisure, but deemed practice at pasture a waste of valuable energy. He early discovered that if he could throw a sufficient "boo" into a sultry heifer by a burst of literally blinding speed in the first few rods before she

---

4 *Ibid.*, 678.

5 I twice spent time on Red Dog's back; the first time was in 1937 and the second in 1940. Red Dog was then in his prime. (The only comparable experience was when I rode Joe Bailey of Gonzales.) In 1937 Jack Casement and I rode much of the meadowland of the Unaweep to bring in the mares. We were at that time hopefully talking about the possibilities of a future Steel Dust registry. Two articles grew out of that visit, Jack's article in *The Western Horseman* entitled "Why a Steel Dust Stud Book," and a little later my article in the same magazine entitled "The Quarter Horse, Then and Now."

The second time I rode Red Dog was when Jim Minnick and I were on the first registration jaunt for the AQHA. If I am not mistaken, Red Dog, No. 55, was in one respect, the second horse registered, since all the others were horses belonging to our first president, Bill Warren.

"het" up, he could trail, point, and pen her any place, from such a leisurely distance that both of them kept cool.[6]

In time Jack sold the Unaweep ranch and moved into northeastern Colorado. Red Dog went with him and lived a full life until he was struck by lightning and killed. Jack's outstanding horses carry Red Dog blood.

Perhaps Frosty should be mentioned next. He was sired by Balleymooney and out of Christina by Springer's Little Joe. Since Christina was a half sister to the dam of Red Dog, Frosty was a three-quarters brothers. Frosty was sold to W. D. Wear, of Wilcox, Arizona. Wear was a well-known Steel Dust breeder and owned Tony, a son of Guinea Pig and grandson of King or Possum. Frosty spent his adolescence on the Unaweep working any stray cattle that came his way. This was one activity he never had to be shown, and would work the critters to any spot in the pasture he chose, regardless of their desires. The more they objected, the better he liked it. After a time Frosty was sold to Chick Logan of Tucson. For years Frosty colts and fillies showed up for the Tucson show and seldom were out of the money.

Another three-quarters brother of Red Dog, Billy Byrne, was sold to Ernest Browning of Wilcox, Arizona. Billy was by Balleymooney and out of Natalie by Springer's New Mexico Little Joe. Ernest Browning is a dyed-in-the-wool cattleman. He said that Billy Byrne was a wonderful using horse and that he had never seen better.[7] Coming from Browning, this is a real tribute. Billy Byrne bred many show winners and rodeo horses. Topper was one of his best-known sons. Another, Sparky, was the champion working horse in California for two years.

When Browning had all of the blood of Billy Byrne he needed, he sold him, and his replacement was a son he called Billy-the-Kid. His dam was Kit, a granddaughter of Possum. She had been an outstanding roping horse before she became a brood mare.

Looking back fifty years, old Concho Colonel left quite a name for himself.

6 "Why We Stick to Steel Dusts," *Western Livestock Journal*, October, 1940, 32.
7 "He Likes the Using Kind," *The Quarter Horse Journal*, September, 1959.

ΩΩΩΩ CHIEF (1916)

Chief was foaled in 1916 or 1917, and he died in 1946. He spent his entire life of twenty-nine or thirty years in the ownership of Claud Stinson of Hammon, Oklahoma. He is buried east of the Stinson barn under some large locust trees, under which he used to stand for hours, drowsily switching flies with his tail, raising a little cloud of dust each time he stamped a foot.

Chief was not a small horse as Quarter Horses are judged. He mounted up well in the withers, and while you would not say he could drink out of a teacup, he did not have a bad head. He had long, strong muscles and good, clean, flat bones. Wear and tear blemished him somewhat, but he had come into the world with good straight legs. Claud claimed he was an excellent saddle animal—fast, intelligent, and not excitable when working cattle or racing. He showed he had been ridden, for he had several saddle scars. His small, round, dark hoofs were noticeable. His pasterns were short, as a working horse's should be.[8]

Fast horses were to the young men in the days when Claud Stinson was growing up what hot-rods are to modern youngsters. Thus Claud developed a good eye for horseflesh. He owned one mare he especially liked because she could fairly fly. Her name was Bess, and Claud enjoyed her speed by matching her in quite a number of races. Then he got married, and somehow he no longer had time to train, match, and race.

He decided to breed Bess and raise some fast horses. The first colt she foaled was sired by Jeff C and was called Little Annie. She got tangled in barbed wire and came out lame. Claud rebred Bess to Jeff C, and the next foal was a filly he named Nettie Stinson. Reed Armstrong bought and raced Nettie at the same time he had Grey Badger.[9] Nettie Stinson ran so well Claud figured that Little

---

[8] This description is taken from notes made by the author when he went to see Chief. *Denhardt Files*, Chief Folder.

[9] Grey Badger, also called Badger, was the sire of Midnight. Reed Armstrong was one of five brothers, all seemingly horsemen. Reed married the daughter of a buffalo hunter, Jake Meek. Reed's brother John trained horses for the King Ranch. Dan Reed trained for Van Vactor who was well known in Oklahoma and Texas for his fast Quarter Horses. Reed was born around 1874 and lived variously at Elk City, Sayre, and lastly at Foss, Oklahoma. *Denhardt Files*, Armstrong Folder.

Annie, who was bred the same way, should be a good brood mare. He bred her to Peter McCue, the best horse he could find. Chief was the result, and he satisfied Claud in every respect.

In a letter written in 1947 and printed as an article, Claud had the following to say about Chief:

> Chief was never raced very much and was never in good running condition at any time he was raced. We would take him out and run him a little and he outrun some of as fast horses as was ever in this country. The last time I run him was at the age of twelve years. I started him in a quarter mile free-for-all at the fall race meet at Seiling, Oklahoma, and again at Canton the next week, running first both times. Chief's best distance was probably 300 or 350 yards. I think Chief could run as fast as any horse could run at the distance, as he was as fast breaker as any horse I've ever seen.
>
> I showed him at-halter at Elk City in the Western Oklahoma Quarter Horse Show in 1941. He took first there, at the age of 24.[10]

While Chief may not have been the greatest of Peter McCue's offspring, certainly his blood has been a steady and beneficial influence to the Quarter Horse as a breed.

Ω Ω Ω Ω MIDNIGHT (1916)

Peter McCue had many grandsons and granddaughters, but none ever did more for the Quarter Horse breed than old Midnight. Midnight's sire, and Peter McCue's son, was Badger. Badger was more famous for his running than for his progeny. It was while he was being handled by two Oklahoma men, Roy Cockran and Reed Armstrong, that he gained his fame. He was kept so busy running that little time was left for siring colts.[11] When a stallion is bred very much, he loses his interest in racing. Only two known progeny of Badger were foaled, one being a mare and the other the stallion Midnight.

Midnight got his name because he was so black as a foal. He

10 "The Story of Chief," *The Quarter Horse*, February, 1947, 4.
11 According to notes made by Helen Michaelis, Armstrong raced Badger (he called him Grey Badger) successfully until he was about six, and then Armstrong sold him to a farmer who wanted a work horse, and so he was gelded. *Denhardt Files*, Armstrong Folder.

65

died almost pure white, as is common for gray horses. As a mature horse he stood 14–2 and weighed 1,150 pounds.

The dam of Midnight was Nellie Trammel.[12] She was sired by Pid Hart and had been bred and raced by Thomas Trammel. Trammel, and his partner Newman, of Sweetwater, Texas, were two of the best-known race horse breeders in Texas during their day. In Texas, they occupied a position very similar to that of the Watkinses of Illinois. In fact, the two establishments often bought or exchanged stock. Dan Tucker and Barney Owens, two of Trammel's best short-horses, were obtained from Watkins.

Nellie Trammel was a clubfooted mare, but she could really move on soft ground and was seldom matched unless the ground was soft. She came into the possession of Jess Cooper and was bred to a common horse. She produced such an outstanding foal by this horse that Cooper decided to take her to the best short-horse he knew and give her a chance. He loaded her up and took her to Badger and talked Reed Armstrong into giving him a service.

When Midnight was born, he looked so good that Jess's brother Al bought half-interest in him. Together they broke and trained Midnight for racing. The first race Midnight ran for important money was a match against an imported horse from Cuba. This was in 1920, and each side put up $500. Midnight scampered across the line an easy winner.

When Reed Armstrong heard that the Coopers had a Badger colt out of the clubfoot mare that was running, he thought he would get some of those Cuban pesos. He had a top sprint horse, A. D. Reed, a son of Peter McCue, and he expected no trouble from the iron-gray Midnight. Midnight, however, had other ideas,

[12] I am inclined to believe the information regarding Midnight's dam much as it was reported by Nelson Nye in "The Story of Midnight," *Quarter Horse*, March, 1948. Helen Michaelis gave a somewhat different version. Since Helen, Nelson, and I interviewed the same people and came up with different stories, the truth will probably never be known. Helen points out that Walter Merrick wrote to H. S. Bissell that he had heard two conflicting stories about Midnight's dam: (1) T. O. Gouse, of Elk City said he was present when they bred the mare that foaled Midnight. He said she was a cripple-footed mare that was never broken but showed wonderful Quarter Horse conformation. Her breeding was unknown. (2) Another fellow told him Midnight's dam was a big chestnut race mare that ran in the Crawford area. She was called the "Negro mare" because she belonged to a Negro. She came from the East and her breeding could not be checked. *Denhardt Files*, Unregistered Studs, A–J.

and he ran away from his uncle, A. D. Reed, and the Coopers had dollars to go with their Cuban pesos.

It was a little rough to match Midnight after a couple of races like this, and the Coopers sold him to Red Whaley. To get a race, Whaley had to approach the best. He challenged the Waggoners, and when he beat the Waggoner horse, the Three D purchased Midnight on the spot. He was then five years old.

He ran for the Waggoner outfit for several years and then was turned out with some mares. Sometime later he was purchased by the JA Ranch, who wanted a little speed with their cow horses. After serving the JA Ranch for several years, he was purchased by Aubray Bowers and taken to his final home. Bowers took good care of the old horse and got several colt crops from him before he died in 1933.

Walter Merrick bought his last horse colt and called him Midnight, Jr. With him he won sixteen straight match races. Midnight, Jr., was out of a Billy the Tough mare.

Old Midnight had his heyday before the formation of the AQHA, but, nevertheless, twenty-three of his get were registered by the association. This indicates the esteem in which Midnight horses were held. Some of the better-known sons of old Midnight were, besides Midnight Jr., Chubby, out of Fourth of July; Rainy Day out of Old Alley; and One Eyed Waggoner, out of a Yellow Wolf mare.

Ω Ω Ω Ω ZANTANON (1917)

Little Joe had many well-known offspring, and Zantanon was not the first nor the last, but he was certainly one of the best. Zantanon's dam was Jeanette by Billy by Big Jim by Sykes Rondo. She was also out of an old Sykes Rondo mare. So Zantanon, with three of four ancestors tracing to Rondo and the other to Traveler, was endowed with the best blood South Texas had to offer. He was also bred by one of the greatest Quarter Horse breeders, Ott Adams, of Alice, Texas. Zantanon was foaled on Adams' ranch on March 27, 1917.

The following year, among the many visitors to see Ott Adams'

67

horses, were a couple of gentlemen from Mexico. One of them bought three horses sired by Little Joe, including Zantanon. The buyer was Erasmo Flores who lived in Nuevo Laredo. As Zantanon grew, he showed signs of speed, and Erasmo's uncle, Eutiquio Flores, purchased the colt. Eutiquio put the colt into training, and Zantanon made him a rich man. He did not, however, take good care of Zantanon. Manuel Benevides Volpe, who admired Zantanon for many years before he was finally able to buy him, told the story in the May, 1947, issue of *The Ranchman*.

First of all I must tell you that he was starved to death all his life. When I bought him in Mexico at 14 years of age he was so weak and poor and full of ticks that he could hardly walk. He made the Mexicans who raced him rich, and their method of training was very hard on the horse. They would walk him on hard gravel streets from downtown to the track, four good miles. Then they would trot him, and gallop him, and jog him at the track until his sweat would dry out. Then they would walk him back home the same four miles. They would not cool him, but instead would tie him under a tree and let him stay tied until four o'clock in the afternoon. Then they would saddle him up again and walk him on the hard gravel streets until dark. They fed him at night on oats and corn for grain and corn fodder for roughage. By that time, he was so tired he would not eat as he should. By the day of the race, he was so poor you could count each and every one of his ribs. By that time, of course, he had no pep but was absolutely dead on his feet. Yet in that condition and with his owner's son weighing 140 pounds and a surcingle (as we did not know the race saddles at that time down here), he could run 300 yards in 15 and 2/5th seconds walking start. I really believe that he was a phenomenon to run at that speed with the weight he carried in his condition.

In my opinion, Zantanon was the fastest horse I have ever seen, and I have seen Lady of the Lake, his half-sister; I have seen Punkin; and I have seen Shue Fly. I still consider Zantanon faster than all of them up to 300 yards for sure and maybe up to a quarter. Zantanon won about eight races off my own father.

John Armstrong, one of the best horsemen and the best rider that I know, said of Zantanon, "He had won his races on his breeding only, as the condition of the horse is such that most any other horse in such condition would not catch a cow."[13]

As you can tell from the foregoing letter published as an article, the fame of Zantanon soon reached back into Texas. His last race was with Conesa, a daughter of Ace of Hearts, whom he beat in 1922. Benevides Volpe went into Mexico and bought the old horse at the age of fourteen from the heirs of Eutiquio Flores.[14] Once Benevides got him back to Texas, Zantanon was given the very best of care for the rest of his life.

Some of Zananon's best-known get include King, Ed Echols, Chico, Cucuracha, San Simeon, Zantanon, Jr., Sonny Kimble, and Quatro de Julio. All of Zantanon's get had superior quality, and their performance in the show ring has been almost as good as in the arena or on the short track.

King, who was made famous by Jess Hankins of Rocksprings, Texas, was undoubtedly Zantanon's greatest son.[15] King was foaled on Benevides' ranch near Laredo on June 2, 1931. When he was a two-year-old, he was sold to Bernie James. When he was a four-year-old, Winn Dubois bought him. In 1937, Jess Hankin purchased him. His best-known son was Poco Bueno.

In Oklahoma, two other sons, Chico and Zantanon, Jr., provided foundation stock for many Quarter Horse breeders. In Arizona the get of still another son, Ed Echols, made their mark, especially on the short track. He sired at least seven AAA register of merit winners.

Benevides kept Zantanon for about ten years, breeding many great horses during that period. When Zantanon was twenty-four, in 1941, Benevides sent him to his friend Alonzo Taylor of Hebbronville. He died soon thereafter on Taylor's ranch.

---

13 "Zantanon," *The Ranchman*, May, 1947, 32.

14 For more on Volpe, see Garford Wilkinson's "M. Benevides Volpe," *The Quarter Horse Journal*, August, 1962.

15 For an excellent article giving more information on Hankins and King see "Jess Hankins, 13th President of the AQHA," *The Quarter Horse Journal*, April, 1964. Of interest—when Winn Dubois owned King, he was standing him for $10.00. That was in 1937. Before King died, there was hardly enough money in Texas to buy a breeding. By 1964, he had 611 registered get in the AQHA. King died at the age of twenty-six in 1958.

69

Ω Ω Ω Ω JOE BAILEY OF GONZALES (1919)

Joe Bailey of Gonzales was born on Dr. J. W. Nixon's ranch near Gonzales in 1919. When he was eight, Dr. Nixon took him to town and traded him for a breeding Jack. J. B. Ellis then bought Joe Bailey for $225, a good price for an unregistered stud in 1927. From that day until his death in 1947, he never left the ownership of Ellis and his brother-in-law, C. E. Dickinson. Joe was never used much except in the stud. The few times he was raced, he showed himself to be an honest twenty-three-second horse.[16]

Joe Bailey's sire was King, or Possum, a full brother to Little Joe. His dam was a daughter of Old Joe Bailey of Weatherford.

Joe Bailey was a dark sorrel, stood just 15 hands, and weighed 1,150 pounds. He had a blaze from just below the poll to the nostrils, and his legs below the knees and hocks were roan, shading to almost white at the hoofs. He mounted up well in the withers, was deep through the heart, and had a tremendous rear end, being well muscled inside and outside of the leg. He was not excessively wide between the front legs and had a good, but not exceptional, head.

It would be impossible even to estimate how many of the descendants of Joe Bailey are registered in the AQHA. He was bred for twenty years. Best estimates by his handlers show he was responsible for at least fifteen hundred live foals. Since this figure includes foals for many years before the AQHA was organized, only a small portion of the early blood came into the association. He lived for about seven years after the AQHA registry was established.

The first of Joe Bailey's get to make a mark in the association record book was Little Joe, Jr. Little Joe, Jr., could do it all. He was bred by Preston Johnson of Waelder, Texas, who took his good mare, Dumpy by Little Dick, to Joe Bailey of Gonzales in 1936 to raise a roping horse. The result was so good that Preston couldn't keep Little Joe. Larry Baumer of Utopia, Texas, and W.

[16] I rode Joe Bailey and let him out at Ellis' request. I may have ridden faster horses, but I can't recall any. You can tell when a horse is really moving because his up and down motion seems to disappear and the wind whistles a somewhat different tune in your ears. Joe Bailey could run.

E. Richardson of San Antonio soon bought him. Larry Baumer took him to Arizona for the show and races in 1942. Tucson at that time was the outstanding area for short racing, and its livestock show was second to none. There Little Joe, Jr., was named grand champion cow horse over a tremendous field. Conformation was the criterion. Too, he showed those who thought he was just another pretty sorrel horse that he could run. He was defeated for the world championship by the great Clabber, but he pushed Clabber every jump from the gate. While racing, he beat the likes of Joe Tom, Chicaro, Bartender, Shadow, and Blueberry Hill. They still talk about the free-for-all he lost to Dan Manners.

Before long, Joe Bailey was purchased by Paul Carney for the Diamond 2 Cattle Company of Arizona and retired to stud. Few of his colts have left the ranch, but some showed up at the race tracks, like Joe Jimmy and Nurse. Mares by Little Joe, Jr., have produced many fast race horses. Perhaps his lasting fame will be as a sire of brood mares.

Joe Bailey of Gonzales died in 1947. He had been to Luling, Texas, breeding some mares, and returned home on May 2. He got down in his stall and was cast. In his struggles he somehow injured himself internally. Mr. Ellis heard the clatter and went promptly and got the old horse to his feet and outside. He seemed all right, so Ellis went to bed satisfied. However, old Joe Bailey of Gonzales died that night under the Texas stars that he had watched for almost twenty-eight years.

Ω Ω Ω Ω RIALTO (1923)

Rialto was bred by Ott Adams. Little Joe figures prominently in Rialto's pedigree, as he does in so many South Texas horses. Little Joe outran Carrie Nation, Rialto's sire's dam, and Little Joe was Rialto's dam's sire.

The race between Carrie Nation and Little Joe was arranged by George Clegg. George raised Little Joe, trained him as a two-year-old, then took him to San Antonio and matched Carrie Nation. Carrie Nation was an outstanding race mare. She was in a class with Della Moore and Pan Zareta. All had either held world records

71

or beaten world record holders while they were running. Carrie Nation had held the five-eighth mile record a number of years. She was sired by Peter McCue.

Rialto's dam was one of Ott Adams' best mares. Her name was Dora du Mar and she was by Little Joe. Her dam was Julia Crowder by Old John Crowder.

Rialto's sire, Billy Sunday, was campaigning in South Texas and making a name for himself by defeating all of the local champions. Occasionally he would lose a race, but always seemed able to win the rematch. When it became difficult to find races for him, Ott Adams bought Billy Sunday, who at that time was in the hands of a man named Peeler.

Rialto was an exception to Adams' usual breeding procedure because his bloodlines were inverted. Rialto's top line contained Peter McCue blood from Billy Sunday, while Rialto's dam, Dora, was pure Billy, being Traveler and John Crowder. Perhaps this is one reason he was willing to sell the chunky sorrel colt so readily to Tom Taylor and Jasper Singleton, the two Negro gentlemen who lived at Kendleton, Texas, a few miles southwest of Houston.

Singleton had been a jockey in his youth and for years had followed the racing circuit, first as an exercise boy and groom, then as a jockey, and occasionally as a trainer. Tom Taylor, distantly related to Jasper, farmed a few acres not far from Kendleton. It was Jasper who wanted a race horse. Once, when he was light enough to jockey, he had ridden in a race against Billy Sunday and had been beaten so easily that ever after he had wanted a Billy Sunday colt to race.

Jasper Singleton was in Alfred in 1926 and visited Ott Adams' ranch. There he saw a three-year-old Billy Sunday colt whose hocks were high and knees were low. His head may have been plain and his throatlatch thick, but there was nothing wrong with the parts that made for locomotion. Ott Adams sold Rialto to Jasper and Tom in 1927, and he was taken to Kendleton, which became his home for much of his life.

Just after they bought Rialto, Jasper had a chance to train; he left Kendleton, and Rialto was never raced. As Taylor later said in a letter to me:

> We never did race Rialto, we just owned him and bred him. He never had a chance to prove himself as a performer. We just started breeding these colored boys' mares and pretty soon the results showed him to be a great sire. We colored people around here would take a Rialto colt and start hunting the race tracks. It wasn't long until they began asking us a lot of questions about where from these horses came, 'cause we won regular with them.[17]

Rialto's fame spread and could have spread farther except that South Texas at that time had several other horses whose owners were white and who had the money to see that they performed and were advertised. Menter Northington had Grano de Oro; George Clegg had Hickory Bill; Raymond Dickson had Paul El; Ott Adams had Little Joe; J. B. Ellis had Joe Bailey.[18]

By the time the AQHA was formed in 1940, John Taylor, Tom Taylor's son, was in charge, and he sold Rialto to the O'Quinns, well-known Quarter Horse breeders of Bammel, Texas. Rialto was an old horse now, and early the following year (1944) he became ill with a throat ailment. O'Quinn took him to Texas Agriculture and Mechanical College's Veterinary Clinic, but Rialto died that August in spite of the best medical care possible. His descendants still carry the deep rich stream of blood the name of Rialto (Río Alto) promised.

Ω Ω Ω Ω JOE HANCOCK (1923)

This is how Joe Hancock was registered in the *Official Stud Book and Registry of the American Quarter Horse Association.*

> 455 JOE HANCOCK—Brn. S. 1923; Tom L. Burnett Estate, Fort Worth, Texas: Sire, John Wilkins by Peter McCue by Dan Tucker; Dam, Unknown. (It is said Joe Hancock's dam was half

---

[17] Denhardt, "The Story of Rialto," *Quarter Horse*, January, 1948, 8.

[18] I doubt if there were many locations that in the 1920's and 1930's could claim as many good Quarter Horses as South Texas. Little Joe, Traveler, and Rondo were making their presence felt.

Percheron. His brilliant racing record and his great colts make this seem unlikely and unimportant.)[19]

Joe Hancock was well proportioned and well balanced. His grandsire, Peter McCue, was 16–2 and weighed 1,430 pounds. Joe Hancock was nearly the same size. Tom Burnett called him the greatest Quarter Horse that ever lived. There is no doubt that he could produce the best—his numerous progeny have proved this.[20]

While the Hancocks were living in Perryton, Walter E. Hancock bought a Peter McCue colt named John Wilkins. He raised several fast colts sired by John Wilkins, but the best colt John Wilkins sired was Joe Hancock. Joe's dam was not one of John Hancock's mares. She was a crossbred mare that had just a little too much size.

There is some evidence that Joe Hancock may have been foaled in 1924. The "It is said" part of his dam's breeding record might be left out; there is enough evidence to prove beyond reasonable doubt that his dam was a half-breed mare.

In a letter written to the author in 1963, Helen Michaelis had this to say about Joe Hancock:

> Some have said Joe Hancock was a freak. Had he been a freak or a sport he would not have been such a strong breeder of outstanding Quarter Horses. The Joe Hancock's have carried on for over thirty-five years, on ranches, in the rodeo arena, and on the race track. Whether one admires draft blood in his Quarter Horse or not, Joe Hancock's descendants look a lot more like Quarter Horses than some 15/16 Thoroughbreds of today that have been registered as Quarter Horses.[21]

Helen went on to say he was a big, rugged horse with lots of speed. That he had the straightest hind legs she could remember, and that he stood almost 15–3 and weighed 1,300 pounds. She was very conservative in the estimate of his size. Then she added

[19] *Official Stud Book and Registery of the American Quarter Horse Association*, I, 1, 72.

[20] John J. Hancock's grandson, Tom L. Hancock of Nacona, Texas, claims Joe Hancock was named for his father who owned the horse from the time he was a yearling until John Ogle began racing him. Ogle named him. Letter dated at Nacona, Texas, on February 4, 1964. *Denhardt Files*, Joe Hancock Folder.

[21] Letter dated at Kyle, Texas, on November 11, 1963. *Denhardt Files*, Joe Hancock Folder.

that he was raced extensively in Texas and Oklahoma and that there was good authority saying he had run the quarter in less than 22 seconds. It is true Joe Hancock was not a Steel Dust type of Quarter Horse—he was too big and coarse—but he was registered for what his colts were and would be.

G. B. Mathis wrote Helen in 1941[22] that Joe Hancock was foaled in 1924, not 1923, at Perryton. He said Walter Hancock was the breeder and owner of both sire and dam. The dam, he said, was sired by a Percheron and out of a good Quarter mare. He added that she was a dark bay with no white on her, being very smooth and well balanced. This jibes well (for the most part) with Walter Hancock's story.[23] John Elbert Ogle, who later raced Joe, gave much the same account. It was Ogle who later established a record on Waggoners' track when he ran Joe a quarter-mile in twenty-two and three-fourths seconds.

Joe was fast, so fast that certain people needed a better chance to cash in on his speed. The best bet was on the Thoroughbred tracks, as parimutuel betting on Quarter Horses was still fifteen or twenty years in the future. Thus, as for many Quarter Horses before and some since, Thoroughbred registration papers were obtained for Joe Hancock. He is listed in *The American Stud Book*.[24] He is registered as Brown Wool. He *was* brown. His foaling date is given as 1925 and his dam as Maggie Murphy. His sire is listed as Wool Winder. Joe had to retire when he matured because he no longer presented the ideal picture of a Thoroughbred.

Joe Hancock built his early reputation on the race track, but his real fame was to come as a sire on a Texas ranch. He was bought for his speed by one of Texas' most astute horsemen, Tom Burnett, and it was on Tom's ranches that he was to spend his last days,

---

22 Letter dated at Stinnett, Texas, on June 9, 1941. *Denhardt Files*, Joe Hancock Folder.

23 With Jim Minnick, I went to Oklahoma in 1940 to see Walter Hancock and John Ogle to get more information on Joe Hancock for the association. We went by way of the Triangle Ranch in Cottle County to see the stallion. For the most part, the story of Joe Hancock as told here follows notes taken on that trip, filled out a little with information sent to the author by Helen Michaelis in a letter dated in Kyle, Texas, on November 16, 1963. *Denhardt Files*, Joe Hancock Folder.

24 The Jockey Club, *The American Stud Book*, XIV, 506.

siring some of the most famous Quarter Horses it has been Texas' privilege to produce.

John Burns, who during Joe Hancock's life managed the Burnett estate, wrote about Joe Hancock:

> Joe Hancock could run and he transmitted his speed quite consistently to his offspring. He was a big horse, heavily boned and muscled and quite well balanced in his conformation, and stood on well set legs. His feet were on the large side, and one could sum him up by saying that he was a big horse, powerfully built, with a lot of speed and action. He would weigh 1450 pounds in just ordinary condition. His offspring were in strong demand as rope horses because of their strength, speed and action.[25]

Joe Hancock lived out his life on the Triangle Ranch of the Burnett estate. As was the custom on most Texas ranches, he was turned out each spring with his band of mares, and it was in July, 1941, while he was in the pasture that he almost severed his left front hoof on a wire. A veterinarian, Dr. Phillip Smith of Abilene, one of the top veterinarians in the country, was called. By the time Dr. Smith saw Joe, the cut was several days old and the screwworms were pretty bad. The injury responded so slowly to treatment that in September Dr. Smith took Joe to Abilene in order to check him daily. He was kept there, improving all the time, until the next spring when he was returned to the ranch where he was needed for breeding purposes. The doctor, however, continued to watch over Joe's foot, making thirteen trips to the Triangle Ranch between April and July. However, after foundering, on July 13, 1943, Joe's good foot gave way on him, causing him to start walking on his bad foot. Finally, it too gave way and Joe Hancock was destroyed on July 29, 1943, about 3:00 p.m. Dr. Smith still has a cannon bone from Joe's cut leg—a memo of one of the all-time-great modern short-horses. In the eyes of the oldtime ranchers, the top mounts were the cutting and steer-roping horses. No horse has produced more top-caliber ranch and rodeo horses than old Joe

[25] Letter dated at Fort Worth, Texas, on October 22, 1963. *Denhardt Files*, Joe Hancock Folder.

Hancock. It is small wonder the real cowmen still revere his name and use his blood.

Ω Ω Ω Ω MARK (1925)

Along with Joe Hancock, Mark must take his place as one of the greatest sires of roping, cutting, and rodeo horses. His grandsire was the Texas horse called King (in Arizona, Possum), a son of Traveler and a full brother to Little Joe. Some Quarter Horse men who knew both horses felt that King was a better individual than Little Joe. The two were about equal in speed and prepotency.

King, or Possum, left many sons and daughters in Arizona, the best-known sons, as previously mentioned, probably being Blue Eyes, Red Cloud, and Guinea Pig. Most of their progeny ended up on ranches in Arizona, New Mexico, and California. A few found their way into quarter racing.

Mark is a line-bred Traveler, his sire being Red Cloud by Possum (King) by Traveler. Mark was bred by Burns Blanton, who lived on a ranch near Wilcox, Arizona. Blanton selected one of his best mares to send over to breed to J. J. Kennedy's Red Cloud. Some records give Mark's dam as Maga by Possum (King), but Helen Michaelis says that Tom Mattart claimed Mark's dam was a McKittrick mare sired by King, a registered Thoroughbred.[26] In the spring of 1925, some twenty-five or thirty miles from Wilcox, Mark was foaled. Blanton named him after his good friend Mark Dubois.

Mark's life was from the start oriented toward cattle. Burns started using him for ranch work as soon as he was broken. He learned to rope almost as soon as he learned to rein. He proved to be gentle and easy to handle. This made it easy to take him to rodeos and also may have had considerable influence on the decision to leave him a stallion. Had he been temperamental or rank, his riders or owners never could have taken him with them. Fortunately, he passed on this gentle spirit to his offspring. It was not long until his services were in demand—as a mount to rope on and

26 *Denhardt Files*, Unregistered Studs, K–Z. See also Nelson C. Nye, *Outstanding Modern Quarter Horse Sires*, 171.

as a sire for prospective colts. Carl Arnold used to rope and tie steers on Mark.

Most of Mark's colts became ranch and rodeo horses and so never received the widespread publicity afforded race horses. They were well known by those who wore high heels and big hats. It was almost a rule that at any western rodeo the man to beat was the one riding a Mark colt. Many consider Mark the greatest roping-horse sire of all time.

6. INFLUENTIAL
THOROUGHBRED BLOOD

I T IS A FACT that a few good Quarter Horses have carried Thoroughbred blood. In a later chapter some of the inherent dangers
of using Thoroughbred blood are discussed. In most cases the
horses mentioned in this chapter were used on Quarter mares primarily to raise race horses, although short speed has always been
an essential characteristic of the Quarter Horse. Intelligent horsemen know that if it is just speed that is wanted, they need go no
further than to the pure Thoroughbred. The Quarter Horse is a
breed because he has certain other features not common in the
Thoroughbred, plus a respectful burst of speed over a short distance. The following horses have influenced the modern Quarter
Horse because they had Quarter blood, not because they had Thoroughbred blood.

Ω Ω Ω Ω UNCLE JIMMY GRAY (1906)

Uncle Jimmy Gray was registered by the Jockey Club but his
progeny had early speed and were the answer to the short-horse
breeder's demands. He was bred in the purple, his sire being Bonnie Joe by Faustus. Interestingly enough, he was a half brother of
Joe Blair, the sire of Joe Reed. He was a sorrel with a blaze and a
white hind foot. C. B. Campbell, his breeder, who lived in Minco,
Oklahoma, owned a little Quarter mare named Betty Campbell,
by Bob Peters, a grandson of Barney Owens, and she was, according to reports, Jimmy's dam. Jimmy was foaled on April 13,
1906. He began his racing career as a two-year-old and ran for
some ten years in races ranging from Canada to Mexico. His career on the tracks can be followed in *Goodwin's Turf Guide*. As a

79

three-year-old, he started seventeen times, was first nine times and out of the money only twice. Two times in Oklahoma City he ran five-eighths in fifty-nine and three-fourths seconds carrying 119 pounds. His best distances were from one-half to five-eighths of a mile. In 1921, he was acquired by the Remount Service, significance of which is explained in Chapter 7, and his real life work began. He was then 15–1 hands high and weighed 1,050 pounds. He was selected by Ed Pfefferling, of Pfefferling Brother's Horse and Mule Barn in San Antonio, and stood for this concern for the rest of his life. He was condemned by Army inspectors in 1929, but at the request of the Pfefferlings, they were allowed to keep him. He died three years later.

To list a few of his progeny well known on the short tracks, there was Major Speck, who could not only run but who produced Lane's Flicka, Major D, and Gallant Maid. Then there was Major Grey, the sire of Silver and Tommy Grey, the sire of Chain Lay. Alamo, the sire of Cyclone, Go Forth, and the grandsire of Twist was also by Uncle Jimmy Gray. My Pardner, who sired Mariposa and the dams of Rosita and Rosalita, were also offspring of Uncle Jimmy Gray. Because of his Thoroughbred breeding, most of his blood came into the Quarter Horse studbook from the distaff side.

Ω Ω Ω Ω OKLAHOMA STAR (1915)

Oklahoma Star was a beautiful mahogany bay with just two white areas on his body—a small star just above the eye line and a left hind foot white through the ankle. He showed his Thoroughbred blood in his general conformation. It was especially noticeable in his ears, head, withers, and long bottom line. He stood about 15 hands and weighed around 1,100 pounds. He showed some short-horse characteristics in his short pasterns and in the sloping rump and heavily muscled rear legs. One would not suspect he was the sire of beautiful model Quarter Horses such as Star Deck, Nowata Star, Osage Star, and the many others. It all goes to show that the physical appearance of the individual producer is no guide to his get.

In 1914, Tom Moore, who lived near Laverne, Oklahoma, took

his favorite mare, Cut Throat, to the Thoroughbred Dennis Reed. Some eleven months later, Cut Throat foaled a long-legged little stud colt with a neat star on his bay forehead. Tom, when he saw the new colt and his fancy star, called him Oklahoma Star, and Oklahoma Star he remained until he died some twenty-seven years later.

Oklahoma Star's sire was Dennis Reed, a Thoroughbred. Cut Throat, his dam, was by Gulliver who was by Missouri Mike. She was out of Money Spinner by Dan Tucker.[1]

Cut Throat was Tom Moore's favorite mare because she was a great race mare, with a reputation covering several states. Laverne is right at the start of the Oklahoma Panhandle, not far from southern Kansas, southeastern Colorado, and northern Texas, all Quarter Horse country. Cut Throat ran so well that eventually she could not be matched, and the only way to get purses was to enter her in the organized races held at the various county and state fairs. To enter, she needed to be registered, and so papers were obtained. Thereafter, she ran on the Thoroughbred tracks as May Matteson.

Oklahoma Star started racing as a two-year-old. Moore had confidence in Star, as he had caught a couple of early-morning workouts in fast time. He decided to trust Star and go for broke. He matched the best right off the bat and had no trouble getting all of his money covered when it was known his untried two-year-old was going to run the great Slip Shoulder 220 yards. Oklahoma Star beat Slip Shoulder. Her owners paid off but were not satisfied. They figured something must be wrong with Slip Shoulder. Kate Bernard was brought in from Texas—the bettors hoping to get their money back from this bay two-year-old. Again Star took the race easily, running a scored 220 in eleven seconds flat. This time, everyone became a believer. It was hard to get anybody who saw this race to bet against Oklahoma Star again.

1 There are different stories about Oklahoma Star's dam, although everyone agrees he was sired by Dennis Reed. Ronald Mason, who owned Star for many years until his death, wrote to me as follows: "Now Bob, as to Oklahoma Star. There has been so much written about him that there is not much to talk about. One fact stands out, he was a hell of a horse regardless of what was the breeding of Cut Throat. The man I bought Star from said she was by Bonnie Joe and I am inclined to believe it." Letter dated in Nowata, Oklahoma, on October 16, 1963. *Denhardt Files*, Oklahoma Star Folder.

For the next dozen years Tom Moore raced Star. He often rode him himself, although he was well over forty and weighed about 150 pounds. He was afraid the gamblers might try to get to his jockey. He rode all of the bigger races, giving up valuable weight, but Star won most of the time. The names of those he out-ran reads like a Who's Who of the short-racing world at the time—Duck Hunter, Henry Star, Jimmy Hicks, Big Jaw, Nellie S and others.

It was not until the 1930's that Star's colts were heard from. He was then owned by Ronald Mason of Nowata, Oklahoma. Most of the colts turned out to be model Quarter Horses, and all were cow horses, with a turn of speed. His fame as a sire first spread among the cowboys. Rodeo performers like Ike Rude, Bob Crosby, Dick Truitt, Jess Goodspeed, and Clyde Burke were riding, or had ridden, his colts and were looking for more. When the revival of interest in Quarter Horses came along, individuals like Star Deck, Pet, Nowata Star, Farmer Girl, Staraway, Topsy, and many others spread his fame far and wide. Here was a case of Thoroughbred blood mixing well with the Quarter Horse.

Ω Ω Ω Ω The Old Sorrel (1915)

The main business of the King Ranch revolves around thousands of head of cattle. Hundreds of saddle horses are required to run the ranch. Most of the cowboys are *vaqueros* of Mexican and Indian descent who have lived on the ranch all their lives. Cattle were made to be worked by horsemen and the King Ranch *vaqueros* are among the greatest. They savvy horses and cows.

The owners of the King Ranch have always been cowmen, who when on the ranch put in a day's work, generally in the saddle. They know and demand good cow horses. Robert J. Kleberg, Jr., the man most responsible for their Quarter Horses, found that the racing Thoroughbred left something to be desired as a cow horse. This is why the ranch started its horse program which eventually resulted in the now famous King Ranch Quarter Horses.

Although Bob Kleberg was not sold on the Thoroughbred as a cow horse the South Texas Billy horse did not fill his eye either. Billy horses were too compact to fit Kleberg's desires, so he looked

82

for a sire of Quarter Horse breeding with which he could perpetuate the qualities he admired in both types. He wanted to eliminate some Thoroughbred characteristics and combine the good features of the Thoroughbred with the temperament, maneuverability and cow sense of the Quarter Horse. Caesar Kleberg, who ran the Canales division of the ranch, saw eye to eye with Bob, and it was Caesar who actually purchased the prototype for the King Ranch Quarter Horses, the horse that was to become known as The Old Sorrel.

The colt was about six months old when Caesar first saw him in 1915. He was sired by Hickory Bill and out of a Thoroughbred mare owned by George Clegg which came from Kentucky. The colt was not delivered to the King Ranch until the fall of 1918, shortly before the end of World War I in Europe.

When the Clegg horse arrived at the ranch, it was named George Clegg after its breeder. However, as the years went by, the *vaqueros* around the ranch just referred to him as "*El Alazán Viejo*" or The Old Sorrel. The name stuck. He was registered as The Old Sorrel. When he was broken, both Bob and Caesar Kleberg rode him until they were satisfied he could do it all. Some of the things they were especially looking for and found were temperament, cow sense, endurance, intelligence, and a good mouth.

Bob Kleberg knew exactly how he was going to breed the horse he wanted. He had been most successful in setting characteristics not long before when he created the Santa Gertrudis cattle.[2] He planned to repeat approximately the same program with The Old Sorrel by selecting outstanding mares. He also had some Quarter mares which he planned to use in his program.

The top colt of the first cross of The Old Sorrel and a Thoroughbred mare was Solis. It must not be assumed that Solis was selected

2 Robert J. Kleberg, Jr., had done the next to impossible by establishing a new breed of beef cattle, the Santa Gertrudis. This was a Brahma-Shorthorn cross that was ideally suited for the hot, damp climate of the Gulf Coast. Before the creation of the AQHA, he was well on the way toward creating his own breed of sorrel cow horse, by crossing the Thoroughbred and the Quarter Horse. When the AQHA was formed, Kleberg joined the association and registered his horses in the Quarter Horse *Official Stud Book*. For an excellent description of the King Ranch activities read *The King Ranch*, by Tom Lea.

immediately from the first colt crop. There had been a continual elimination process which Kleberg supervised. The bottom half were gelded and put in with saddle horses. The top half were carefully broken and ridden by the family and the other top horsemen. Then they were ranked in all their activities. Selected fillies were also put through this routine. When the top three or four stallions were selected, each was given a carefully screened group of half sisters and some hand-picked Quarter mares for an outcross.

When the foals of this second cross arrived, they went through the same process of culling and selection. It was then decided that Solis was best. In 1940, when the first registrations were being made by the association, eight sons and grandsons of The Old Sorrel were being bred to bands of mares who were daughters and granddaughters of The Old Sorrel. Something like three hundred mares were involved in the program, and another five hundred of both sexes were still being tested and culled. It was from these groups that the horses were selected to be registered. Just over one hundred were registered. Some of the more familiar sires of the horses registered were Solis, Tino, Cardinal, Ranchero, and Little Richard. There were also ten or twelve mares by Chicaro. In almost every case, The Old Sorrel was the sire or grandsire.[3]

As time passed, some great horses were produced, all bred about the same way. Take Wimpy, for example. He was half Quarter Horse and half Thoroughbred, close to what Bob Kleberg wanted. To define Wimpy's breeding in another way, a son of The Old Sorrel was bred to a daughter of The Old Sorrel. The son had a Thoroughbred dam and the daughter a Quarter Horse dam.

This breeding employed by Kleberg may seem a little close, or

[3] The officials making the first inspection trip to the King Ranch were Jim Minnick, Lee Underwood, and I. We were escorted on our rounds by Bob Kleberg, Dr. J. K. Northway, and Lauro (Larry) Cavazos. Dr. Northway is internationally famous as a veterinarian and was Kleberg's consultant on livestock matters. He had been intimately connected with both the Santa Gertrudis and the Quarter Horse programs. Cavazos was the ranch foreman. He knew the history and location of every animal on that ranch. Incidentally, he was one of the two or three outstanding horsemen I have ever known. Reference is made here to the following works by the above men: Robert J. Kleberg and A. O. Rhoad, "The Development of a Superior Family in the Modern Quarter Horse," *The Journal of Heredity*, August, 1946; Dr. J. K. Northway, "Like Begets Like," *The Cattleman*, September, 1965. Another excellent treatise on that ranch's horses is "King Ranch Horses," *Cattleman*, September, 1940.

tight, as inbreeding is sometimes called. It may be tight for the average breeder with only thirty or forty mares, but when undertaken by a master breeder and geneticist like Bob Kleberg—using several hundreds of mares—it works. Proper individuals and careful culling insures success, and the desired characteristics are set.

Other examples of Kleberg's breeding were Peppy, who won the Fort Worth show in 1940, and Macanudo, who won the Kingsville show a few months before the Fort Worth show. Peppy was by Little Richard by The Old Sorrel and out of a daughter of Cardinal by The Old Sorrel. Macanudo was by The Old Sorrel and out of a Hickory Bill mare. All were top horses. It is to the credit of The Old Sorrel that his colts have been outstanding in all activities, roping, cutting, racing, and showing. They are all-round horses.

Ω Ω Ω Ω JOE REED (1921) AND JOE REED II (1936)

Joe Blair was a Thoroughbred and a fast one. One of his greatest races was run against Pan Zareta[4] at Juárez, Mexico, in 1916. Although Joe Blair was beaten in this race, it was a long way from a disgrace, as Pan Zareta set the world's record that day and Joe Blair covered three and one-half furlongs in thirty-nine seconds. Whether or not it has ever been done again is open to question. Joe Blair was by Bonnie Joe who was by Faustus by Inquirer by Leamington, so that he had in his sire line some of the fastest Thoroughbred blood in the world.

Joe Blair was the sire of Joe Reed, and his dam was the incomparable Della Moore.[5] When she was in San Antonio in 1920 she was bred, without the knowledge of her owner, to Joe Blair. For about a year she was out of racing, and the horse colt that she foaled was named Joe Reed.

Della Moore's owner, John Lindsey, who most anxious to have her racing again, and so Joe Reed was taken from her at a very

---

4 Had Pan Zareta bred like she ran she would have had a chapter in this book. She was named for the beautiful daughter of the mayor of Juárez and was bred and raised by one of Texas' most prominent cattle families. As John Hendrix wrote in the September, 1945, issue of *The Cattleman*, "In the short span of her meteoric career, covering the years from 1912 to 1917, she set records on race tracks of America that stand unbroken to this day." She lies enshrined in the infield of the race track in New Orleans.

5 For more on Della Moore, see Chapter 4.

85

early age. When Lindsey returned after racing Della for a season, he found Joe Reed, a stunted yearling colt, turned loose in a cotton field, practically starved to death. It wasn't long, however, before Joe Reed had an opportunity to show whether or not he could run. He could. The main trouble with Joe was that he couldn't run far enough. Most races at that time were being run one-half or five-eighths of a mile, which was a little too much for Joe. As a result of his inability to run out, he was soon sold to J. W. House, of Cameron, Texas, who then owned him for many years. He was purchased by Dr. J. J. Slankard, of Elk City, Oklahoma, in 1938. Dr. Slankard owned the horse until his death. It was while he was in the hands of House that Joe Reed II and Red Joe of Arizona were bred. It was while Dr. Slankard owned him that Joe Bob, Catachu, and Reed McCue were foaled.

Joe Reed was foaled in 1921 and died on May 19, 1947. Some of the better-known Joe Reed colts were Joe Reed II, Joe Darter, Little Fanny, Two Timer, Sue Reed, Catachu, Red Joe of Arizona, Ann Burnett, Hi-Tone, Reed McCue, Joe Sunday, Joe Bob, Jim Reed, Little Abner McCue, and Betty Wood.

In 1935, Joe Reed, who was then owned by J. W. House, was bred to one of House's best mares, Nelleen. Nelleen was by Fleeting Time by High Time by Ultimus by Commando by Domino. She was out of Little Red Nell who was by Old Billy. Bert Wood, of Tucson, Arizona, who had been keeping his eye on Joe Reed, decided that Nelleen's foal by Joe Reed was just the horse he wanted. In October, 1941, Bert bought the horse and called him Joe Reed II. At the time he was unbroken and a five-year-old.

Bert Wood broke Joe Reed II himself, working cattle with him day in and day out. It wasn't until 1943 that Bert decided he might have some fun running Joe. However, he was not able to give him the kind of training that was really needed to make a champion, but he got him ready for the Tucson speed trials the best he could. He had bad luck and got Joe partially crippled, but he went ahead and raced him. Joe came out on the track with a limp, and looked around seeming to wonder where he was. Frankie Figueroa was up. Joe won that first race by half a length, and the official time was twenty-three and three-tenths seconds. His second race was on Sunday, February 14, 1943. Here he had competition for the first time. In the same field with him were Chicaro, Domino, Arizona Girl, Red Racer, and Pay Dirt. Because of his foot, Joe had not had an opportunity to be exercised; yet he won this race doing a quarter in twenty-two and eight-tenths.[6] His third and last race was run the following Sunday in the championship speed trials, a quarter of a mile open championship for stallions. Joe's foot was still bad; he had not been exercised; the greatest horse of the day was running against him, the world's champion Clabber. Nevertheless, Joe ran the race, beating Clabber by half a head, he received a tremendous ovation.

Joe Reed II was shown in many halter classes. He twice won the heavy-weight stallion class and in 1944 was grand champion cow horse. However, it was as a stallion that Joe had his greatest success. By 1947, Joe's services, even at $100 stud fee, were in such demand that Bert Wood had to turn away many mares. Among the many great Joe Reed II foals are Leo, Bill Reed, Little Sister W, Bull's Eye, and Whisper W.

Joe Reed II was bred to Little Fanny in 1940 and produced the outstanding sorrel horse Leo. Little Fanny was by old Joe Reed, so that both Leo's sire and dam were by the old horse. Little Fanny's dam was Fanny Ashwell, who was sired by a Thoroughbred and out of Fanny Richardson. Little Fanny was bred by J. W. House and foaled in Cameron, Texas, in 1937. She was raced successfully, but her greatest value was as a brood mare. She was the mother of seven outstanding foals: Leo, Bill Reed, Ashwood, Tick Tack, Tucson, Little Sister W, and Sassy Time.

Joe Reed and his sons have contributed much to the Quarter Horse, and their descendants are noted for their speed, their good heads, and their stylishness.

Ω Ω Ω Ω FLYING BOB (1929)

The greatest sire of running Quarter Horses during the revival of

6 Joe Reed II was "Horse of the Year" in Quarter racing circles in 1943. For more, see *Racing Quarter Horses*, written in 1943, for the Southern Arizona Horse Breeders Association by Melville Haskell.

short racing, which occurred in the 1940's, was Flying Bob. The proof is in the records of the American Quarter Racing Association. Lucky, a bay gelding by Flying Bob, held the 220 record of twelve and two-tenths seconds. Lady Lee, by a son of Flying Bob, was a co-holder of the 330 yard record of seventeen and four-tenths. The co-holder of the 350 record of eighteen and two-tenths was Punkin, a Flying Bob filly. The 440 record was held by Queenie, also by Flying Bob.

Flying Bob was unbeatable when crossed on Louisiana mares sired by Old D. J., as the great Louisiana short-horse stallion Dedier was commonly called. It was he who put the Louisiana Cajuns into the horse business in the early 1900's. Later, when his fillies were crossed by Flying Bob a whole family of short-horses was created that rocked Texas and the Southwest. It was necessary for Texans to go to Louisiana and buy Flying Bobs in order to stay in the race horse business.

The story of Flying Bob really goes back to John Dial of Goliad, Texas. He bought Chicaro, who was in New Orleans in 1928, and brought him to Goliad. The first night was spent in Abbeville, and while there Chicaro was bred to Zerengue's Belle, who, in due time, foaled Flying Bob. Chicaro was by imported Chicle, and Flying Bob was not Chicaro's only son who produced short speed. Chicaro's Bill (out of a Little Joe mare) was responsible for Chicaro, Arizona Girl, and Flicka, while Tony McGee, by Chicaro, sired Peanut. Daughters of Chicaro also produced Don Manners, Maggie (Chovasco), and Pokey.

When mature, Flying Bob was a large, beautifully formed dark bay horse, not as large as his sire, but carrying the same rounded perfection of body and limb. He stood 15–1 and weighed close to 1,200 pounds. Like his sire, he typified the sprinting Thoroughbred.

Flying Bob was widely bred in Louisiana, and when horses like Punkin, Queenie, Dee Dee, Black Beauty, Bay Annie, Effie, Lucky, Danger Boy, and other Louisiana-bred Flying Bobs came to Texas it was not long until Flying Bob himself followed. He died in Richmond, Texas, in 1946. No other sire of short-horses could equal him during this period of short racing and none was better until the advent of Three Bars many years later. None have equaled him in producing Quarter Horse conformation. Mares like Punkin, Effie, and Queenie and stallions like Dee Dee left little to be desired by the better Quarter Horse breeders. There have been few horses carrying as much Thoroughbred blood as Flying Bob who produced Quarter Horse type as well as he.

Ω Ω Ω Ω My Texas Dandy (1929)

The story of My Texas Dandy starts with Mr. C. F. Myers who lived in Ellinger, Texas. The family always had a few good horses, and one of their best was named Sadie May, generally abbreviated to Sadie M. Sadie M was a short-horse, but she ran with some success up to one-half and five-eights of a mile. When she began to slow down, Myers took Sadie May to the neighboring town of Schulenburg to be bred.

The sire of Sadie was Little Dick and her dam was a bay Thoroughbred mare named Nellie, sired by the Thoroughbred Panmure. C. F. Myers had seen Porte Drapeau, who was owned then by Dr. A. J. Clark of Schulenburg, and Myers like the horse, so it was to Porte Drapeau that he took Sadie in 1926.

The spring following, Sadie dropped a sorrel stud colt with a big blaze down his face and one hind foot white above the fetlock. His stocky build and smooth muscling showed his Quarter Horse heritage. As he matured he reverted more to the Thoroughbred and lost his original chunkiness. When Clay Myers, C. F. Myers' son, first saw the colt, he exclaimed, "Boy howdy, is he ever built!" "Boy Howdy" stuck, and that was the colt's first name. His name was changed later—to honor or to collect some reflected glory of another Porte Drapeau colt that was burning up the eastern Thoroughbred tracks. This half brother, that became momentarily famous, was named "My Dandy," and so Myers decided to call his young horse "My Texas Dandy." My Texas Dandy remained on the Myers' ranch until he was old enough to go to the tracks.

In 1928, My Texas Dandy was loaded up and hauled to Hondo, Texas, to be under the supervision of Dr. Henry Mayer. Here he was broken and trained for the tracks by the man who took care of Mayer's horses, Charlie Brenham. When the colt was ready, he was taken to La Grange, New Braunfels, and other adjacent tracks to race. He was no "My Dandy" and attracted very little notice because he did not win any races. Since there is always a tendency to play up the racing prowess of great stallions, we may assume My Texas Dandy was not much of a race horse. Will Hysaw, the colorful, colored race horse buff who ran the gauntlet from jockey to trainer to owner, and who had such close contact with all the short-horses for fifty years, explained My Texas Dandy this way: "Well suh, he would start like a shot but run blind."[7] The fact was that My Texas Dandy never learned to navigate the small "bull-pens," the half-mile circular tracks that were common in Texas at the time. When he started to run he would go right through the outside guard rail if not pulled up.

It soon became apparent that he would not be a race horse, and so he was sold to J. C. Smith. Smith took My Texas Dandy out to his father's ranch at Big Foot, Texas. Ed Bateman quoted Smith as follows:

> He may have run so fast that he scared himself, that's how fast that horse could go. Then he had a bad scar on his leg. It was all healed well when I got him but it may have hurt him when he got up full steam. Or it may have been just like it looked from the side lines—he just lost interest in the race and couldn't see any point in running after he passed every other horse ahead of him. I never saw him win a race but I heard of one he won at Cuero when the jockey just threw the reins over his head and beat him in. That's the only race I ever heard of him winning.[8]

When My Texas Dandy was a five-year-old, Clyde Smith began to breed him, and in 1932 Colonel Clyde, named after Smith, was foaled. In 1933 Captain White Sox was foaled. Four years later an Uncle Jimmy Gray mare foaled Clabber. Ginger Rogers was also out of Meanie, an Uncle Jimmy Gray mare.

[7] Ed Bateman. "The Story of My Texas Dandy," *The Quarter Horse*, October, 1948, 8.
[8] *Ibid.*

Before any of these colts had time to become famous, Smith sold My Texas Dandy to Winn of Uvalde, who in turn sold him to Carroll Thompson of Devine, Texas. Thompson owned Ginger Rogers and liked her so well he decided to buy both her dam and sire. He bought them in 1939. R. C. Tatum of Junction, Texas, took his good mare Streak, by Lone Star, to My Texas Dandy in 1941. She then foaled Texas Dandy, named after his sire, and later this horse was made famous by Tom Finley of Arizona. In 1941, Thompson sold My Texas Dandy to George Herndon of North Uvalde, who owned the old horse until his death. Besides the above-mentioned stallions, the following get of My Texas Dandy gained some fame: Free Silver, Golden Slippers, Chew, Hot Shot, Little Texas, Look Out, Nancy Hanks, Oscar, Texas Star, Pepper, Shadow (sire of Domino), and Texas, Jr.

Ω Ω Ω Ω Clabber (1936) and Colonel Clyde (1932)

Clabber is without doubt My Texas Dandy's greatest son. Not only did he have a fabulous personal career but his sons and daughters have likewise been outstanding, and they and their progeny are most active. Clabber is the original "iron horse" of the modern Quarter Horse breed. He was owned most of his life by A. A. "Ab" Nichols of Gilbert, Arizona, who went to Big Foot, Texas, in 1938 and bought Clabber, selecting him because he liked his looks and because his dam was by Uncle Jimmy Gray.

Nichols took the colt to his ranch and the boys were soon roping calves on the colt, who looked very much like his sire except that instead of a blaze he had an elongated star between his eyes and his hind foot had less white on it. He took to calf roping as if he had been born doing it. The calves looked like they were running in deep sand, Clabber caught up with them so fast. It wasn't long before he was being matched, and he won most of his races.

It was at this time that the "iron horse" title was pinned on Clabber. Ab Nichols did not go for training—just regular work and lots of it. As far as bandages, liniment, blankets, and a clean stall went, Nichols just didn't see any sense in it. He claimed that his horses could outrun the pampered horses, that smelled like a

91

drugstore, any day in the week and twice on Sundays. And Clabber generally did. While Ab Nichols owned Clabber, he ran him at all of the regular meets at Tucson, matched him almost any place, used him at stud an average of one hundred times a year. Clabber put his riders in the money in both steer-roping and calf-roping at any rodeo within trailing distance.

It is true that Clabber was not a picture horse, but he had everything but looks. Even looks seemed unimportant after he beat in a race, won in a roping, or sired a beautiful colt. Melville Haskell said it well in 1941 when he wrote:

> Clabber is a horse of great power—he seems to thrive on rough treatment. During his racing career he has served about 100 mares a year, been used as a race horse and a rope horse, been turned out to pasture and then taken up and hauled several hundred miles in a trailer to race, without resting, and then been hauled home the same day and again turned out to pasture. In spite of all this he is one of the most consistent performers on the short tracks.[9]

Clabber was foaled on Frank Smith's ranch at Big Foot, Texas, but there seems to be some confusion over his breeding. All agree he was sired by My Texas Dandy, but his dam's breeding has been given several ways. At the present time the AQHA carries his dam as Blondie S, by Lone Star and out of Emory Goldman by Captain Joe. The records of the American Quarter Racing Association and Mel Haskell, who was working entirely independent of the AQHA at that time, had Clabber listed as being out of Golden Wheel by Uncle Jimmy Gray. Golden Wheel's dam was a mare by Possum.[10]

Clabber went to the Eagle Pass races in 1941. He ran three quarter-mile races in one day, the last two only an hour apart, and each in 23 seconds, and he won all three.

It was interesting to speculate what would happen if some of the modern pampered short-horses were expected to do this. The last race of the day was the feature race, in which Clabber outran

---

9 *Racing Quarter Horses*, 1943, 15.

10 I was secretary of the AQHA when Clabber's application for registration was received. I registered him as number 507 and gave his breeding according to the original application submitted by A. A. Nichols, which listed his dam as Golden Wheel by Uncle Jimmy Gray—second dam Emory Goldman.

horses like Balmy L, Little Joe, Jr., and Nobody's Friend, to win the event and to become the talk of the race meet. No little wampum changed hands on that race—most of it leaving Texas and going to Arizona.

Later that same year Clabber became the World's Champion Quarter Horse, an honor awarded by the American Quarter Racing Association. His closest competitors for the honor were Little Joe, Jr., and War Chief. In the race that cinched the championship, he carried 135 pounds. He was fractious at the gate, and so Jake Myers, the starter, had a rope put through his bit. When the flag was dropped Clabber moved faster than the men holding the rope. He sent them sprawling and knocked himself to his knees, sending the jockey sliding forward. Clabber scrambled up to his feet with the rope dragging and flapping behind and his jockey desperately trying to get back off his neck and on to the saddle. Clabber did not like the idea of being left at the post. He caught the field and led at the finish. The start, from an open gate set back of the line, was timed from a flag, and as a result cannot be compared with modern times. He was clocked in twenty-two and two-fifths seconds in spite of the starting handicap. Later he ran a race in twenty-two and four-fifths seconds from a regulation gate. Until Shue Fly came on the scene, he was the best of the short racers.

The meeting between Shue Fly and Clabber was inevitable, as was later the meeting between Shue Fly and Miss Princess. When Shue Fly and Clabber tangled, there was a world of difference in the rivals. Shue Fly was beautifully cared for and had been brought along slowly for this race, and she was ready. Clabber, battered up from years of breeding, racing, and rodeoing, was brought out of the pasture and put into the starting gate. He was beaten by a neck. A real champion took the championship from him. He was still plenty good. That same winter he lowered the Tucson track record for 350 yards to eighteen and two-fifths seconds.

Clabber's racing days were about over, but he still continued to do his share of the ranch work and to service all mares that came his way. His better get seemed to come from daughters of Possum. This cross was responsible for Buster, Jeep B, Chester C, Flicka,

93

Tonta Gal, and Brown Lady. When Frank Vessels bought Clabber he had a variety of mares and Clabber did well on all of them. They included Clabber Lady V, Clabbertown G, Wagon N, Clabberita, Clabbers Image, and Clabber II. Clabber died in the ownership of Frank Vessels, in 1947, at Los Alamitos, California.

Ω   Ω   Ω   Ω

Colonel Clyde never achieved the fame of his half brother Clabber. Colonel Clyde's dam was a sorrel mare of Traveler blood and her foal by My Texas Dandy grew into a beautiful horse from the throatlatch back. His head was a typical My Texas Dandy—plain. When full grown, he stood 15 hands and weighed 1,100 pounds in working flesh. His first race was a neighborly affair, because his breeder's and Frank Smith's ranches adjoined. Colonel Clyde was matched against his half brother, Captain White Sox, for 350 yards. Clyde won by a length. In his first race on a circular track he took after his sire and ran straight to the fence, stopping barely in time.

Colonel Clyde eventually came into the ownership of Ab Nichols of Arizona, who liked him so well that he later bought two more colts by My Texas Dandy—Lucky and Clabber. John Bowman, of rodeo fame, saw Colonel Clyde and decided that he must have him for a rodeo horse, and he succeeding in buying him from Nichols in 1938. Once Bowman had Colonel Clyde, the horse became famous in rodeo circles. Colonel Clyde, Baldy, and Bullet were the greatest rodeo horses of all time. Baldy may have been a little better as a calf horse and Bullet a little better as a steer horse, but Colonel Clyde was good at roping calves, steers, team roping, or dogging. He won money for his riders in all of these events. Colonel Clyde, while owned by Bowman, went to every major rodeo in the country. He was roped on at Cheyenne in 1938 and 1939; also at Pendleton and Salinas the same years. Bowman won the steer-roping on him, and Homer Pettigrew, a world's champion bulldogger, regularly dogged and calf-roped on him. In spite of his competitive heart he was gentle, and the Bowman children rode him when he was home between rodeos. He was always a favorite with the crowd. They loved to see him backed into a chute, watching and waiting for the animal to be turned loose, his ears working and treading with his forefeet. When the flag was down, he was off.

Colonel Clyde was never bred as heavily as Clabber, but his breeding record is very good. The best-known mare he sired was probably Prissy, who outran all of the best horses of her day, including those like Miss Bank, Queenie, and Blondie. She set the world's record for 350 yards in 1946. She was killed in a tragic accident along with her jockey at Eagle Pass in 1947.

Colonel Clyde's best-known horse was probably Decoration. Decoration was a crack cutting horse, and John Bowman, his breeder, won the All-Around-Cowboy title on him at Pendleton in 1945. In 1946 Bowman and Decoration again won the steer-roping at Pendleton and the calf-roping at Reno.

Bowman eventually sold Colonel Clyde, and he came into the ownership of Vic Le Grande of Williams, California, who registered him with the AQHA. Later in 1946 he was sold to Don and Neal Townsend of Danville, California, who owned him when he died.

Ω Ω Ω Ω PLAUDIT (1930)

Plaudit has the unique distinction of reflecting glory on two breed associations, the Quarter Horse and Palomino. Plaudit was a late colt, being foaled on July 8, 1930. Tom Mills, of Meeker, Colorado, was his breeder. Mills was a good friend of Coke Roberds and had some of Roberds blood in his Quarter Horses. After Plaudit was foaled, Coke Roberds came by Mills's place, and on seeing Plaudit, he liked him so well he bought him on the spot. He paid Mills $250 for the colt, a huge sum for 1930, a depression year. A Ford roadster did not cost much more.

When Plaudit was a yearling, another friend of Coke Roberds, J. W. Shoemaker, of Watrous, New Mexico, took a liking to the colt. Shoemaker had always been partial to the palomino color, and when it was on a really good individual, such as Plaudit, he could not resist the temptation to buy. Shoemaker kept him for several years and then sold him to Waite Phillips who owned the

95

famous Philmont ranch in New Mexico. Some years later, the ownership of the ranch and the horses, which included Plaudit, were transferred to the Boy Scouts of America. The scouts had little use for a stallion so he was sold to Hal Cooper of Woodward, Oklahoma. Cooper later sold Plaudit to Frank Burns of Alamosa, New Mexico, who in turn sold him to R. W. Roskelly of Fort Collins, who sold him to Leon Harms of Albquerque. Plaudit (QH) was sired by King Plaudit (TB) and his dam was Colorado Queen by Old Nick. Her dam was a mare by Silvertail. King Plaudit was sired by Plaudit (TB) and his dam was Wild Thistle. His grandsire was Himyar.

Plaudit's golden color came from his dam, Colorado Queen. She was an outstanding yellow Quarter mare, by Nick by Old Fred. Old Fred was also a palomino.

Waite Phillips is supposed to have said, after observing Plaudit's get for the ten years he was at the Philmont, that of all the horses he ever owned Plaudit was the most outstanding, not only as a sire but as a performing horse. Phillips in his day owned thousands of horses, so this is rare praise.

Plaudit looked to be the half-breed he was. He stood fifteen hands high and weighed a little over 1,000 pounds. He was a beautiful palomino color with a white mane and tail. He had three white legs, the right front to the fetlock, the right rear to the pastern, and the left rear about two thirds of the way to the hock. He had a deep shoulder, a short ear, and a kind eye.

His greatest son from the point of view of the Quarter Horse breeder was, without doubt, Question Mark. He, too, was a beautiful palomino, and he had two white hind legs to the hocks, and a crooked blaze on his face that gave him his unusual name. His ability made him a great short race horse, and his beautiful conformation placed him in the blue and purple ribbons at almost every show he attended. He ran a scored quarter in twenty-one and four-fifths seconds and three-eighths mile in thirty-three and one-fifth seconds. His best-known race was at Trinidad, where he ran in a three-horse race and defeated two of the best short-horses of his day, Joe Lewis and Shue Fly. There were bets at every eighth pole, and since Question Mark led all the way, he won all bets. He popped a sesamoid bone in his left front foot and went lame, but because he had "heart," he continued running and outgamed his competition to the wire. He could never run again. However, his progeny, such as My Question, Grey Question, Savannah G, and Osage Red carried on his tradition of speed. Question Mark was bred on the Philmont ranch by Waite Phillips and foaled in 1937. His dam was a Thoroughbred mare by the name of Pepito.

Another well-known son of Plaudit was Hank Wiescamp's Scooter W. He was a sorrel colt and, like Question Mark, was foaled in 1937. Scooter was a typical Plaudit, a beautiful individual, and winner of many horse shows. He also could run and qualified AA with the AQRA. His dam was Saucy Sue. Saucy Sue's sire was a Philmont ranch Thoroughbred and her dam a Quarter mare, a granddaughter of Rainy Day.

Plaudit's place in history is secure because of the quality and ability of his sons and daughters, regardless of which breed registry they entered.

7. MIXING
THOROUGHBRED BLOOD

THE HISTORY of the Quarter Horse and the Thoroughbred are so interwoven that no serious work on the Quarter Horse would be complete without an attempt to point out the influence and the danger of this close association.

The author is not critical of the Thoroughbred horse, the greatest runner the world has produced. He does, however, criticize the use of Thoroughbred blood when breeding Quarter Horses. Quarter Horse breeders who do use Thoroughbred blood will undoubtedly point out that many of the horses taken up in this book were race horses with Thoroughbred blood. Some were; some were not. In no case is a horse discussed because he could run or because he had Thoroughbred blood. The only criteria used was the excellence of his offspring. A breeder most usually follows the prosaic law, that like begets like. However, rules of breeding do not apply to the really great horses of a breed. They are acts of God.

Ω Ω Ω Ω No Cold Blood

The Quarter Horse, like the Thoroughbred, may be designated a "hotblood." The purest of the pure hotbloods and the original is, of course, the Arab. Both the Quarter Horse and the Thoroughbred have some outside blood. Neither is "thoroughly bred" in the sense that they have only Arabian blood.

During the Middle Ages, the knights of Europe rode the descendants of great, forest-type horses—distinguished by size, massive bone, and broad feet. They averaged 16 hands or better in height and were characteristically marked by long hair or feather from the fetlock to the knee joint. Horses from the Flanders coun-

98

try were particularly sought after, and during this period the Flemish horse was considered the ideal charger for the heavily armored knight. In England the "Great Horse," or "Black Horse," was used and often crossed with Flemish horses. These massive equine chargers proved themselves ideal for carrying the tremendous weights necessary when mounted by the medieval knights in full armor. The horses also had plates of their own to pack. Our modern breeds of heavy coach and draft horses carry the blood of these great horses—breeds such as the Belgium, Shire, Clydesdale, and Percheron. They form the nucleus of the modern "coldbloods."

The hotblooded horse is the clean-legged horse that had its origin in the dry, open country of Asia and Africa, and included the Arab, Barb, and Turk. They were small horses, averaging from 13–2 to 14–2 hands in height and characterized by small size, short hair, and clean legs. They were introduced into Europe by two routes, one from Asia direct, encouraged by the Crusaders, and the other by way of the Iberian Peninsula.

These small horses were introduced into Spain by the Mohammedan conquest of that country in the eighth century. The Moorish invasion brought much more than horseflesh. Of special interest was the new style of horsemanship known as *a la jineta*. This replaced the old seat and saddle of the armored knight who rode with long stirrups in the *a la brida* manner.[1] A similar saddle and style of riding, as well as the Moorish neck reining and palate bit, are still in use in our West today, modified somewhat by ten centuries of use by the Spanish, Mexicans, and Americans. In other words, the Indian horses owned by the Cherokees and Chickasaws were in their own way just as "thoroughly bred" as the English horses imported into America by the colonists. The only difference was that the Indian horses were brought to America by the Spanish instead of by the English.[2]

The horse you hear most often referred to as a hotblood is the

[1] For a more detailed discussion of the *a la brida* and *a la jineta* method of riding see Cunninghame Graham's *The Horses of the Conquest*, 17–21.

[2] Early horsemen in America thought very highly of the horses imported from Spain. Edgar, for example, in his *General Stud Book* lists many horses from Spain, Gibraltar, and North Africa. Horsemen also spoke highly of the Indian horses—as is brought out in Chapter 1.

99

Thoroughbred. This is proper, although the definition does not limit the term exclusively to him. Thoroughbreds trace back in direct male line to three horses from the East introduced into England; they were the famous Byerly Turk, the Darley Arabian, and the Godolphin Barb. However, there would be no question of the Thoroughbred's origin even if all studbooks were destroyed and his pedigree unknown. His clean-legged frame, moderate stature, his conformation, and temperament—all serve to identify him as Oriental in origin and to distinguish him from the descendants of the heavy horses of Europe, who were cold-blooded.

The Barbs, Turks, and Arabs were, and are, small horses, averaging around 14 hands and weighing under 1,000 pounds. The original horse of Northern Europe was 16 hands or better and weighed well over 1,400 pounds. Care, feed, and certain crosses have tended to increase the size of all modern breeds by a hand or better, and their weight has increased proportionately. But basically, the coldblood is a heavy horse; the hotblood, a light horse. Size also includes more than mere bulk. It includes bone, which in the draft horse is coarse and large and needs to remain so in order to support the tremendous weights.

The underpinning of the Oriental, or hotblood, is clean, slender, and smooth, with no excess hair on the fetlock or the back of the cannon. Their hoofs are small, round, tough, and wellformed. Chestnuts, those horny growths found on the inside of horses' legs just above the knee and below the hock, are very inconspicious and occasionally even missing from the hind legs of hotbloods. The forest horse of Northern Europe and his descendants, the draft horses of today, display chestnuts on all four legs. Draft horses also have large hair growths on the fetlocks, and this growth or feather often extends up the back of the cannon to the knee or above. Their feet are also immense, big, and round like a dinner plate, the better to get them over the marshy lands of their natural habitat.

The temperament, or spirit and disposition of the Arab–Barb group, is energetic, lively, affectionate, and quick. They are higher strung and given to quicker reaction, both muscular and emotion-

100

al, than are their cold-blooded cousins. The draft breeds are more phlegmatic, have a strong tendency to be lazy, and are slower in reacting to stimuli. Hot-blooded animals are continually showing their interest in what goes on about them. Each movement in the grass at the side of the road, each time a bird flies by, or whenever the wind brings a change of scent, his interest is immediately aroused.

It should not be necessary to contrast the two types further to give a clear picture of a hotblood. Every owner of a Quarter Horse or Thoroughbred knows that his favorite breed is a hotblood in every sense of the word. His conformation, his bodily characteristics, his performance, and his temperament are all inherited from Oriental forebearers.

Ω Ω Ω Ω "Bulldogs"

There was a day when the name "Steel Dust," or the adjective commonly used to indicate Steel Dust type—"bulldog," signified the difference between the Quarter Horse and the Thoroughbred. Quarter Horse characteristics were something to be proud of, to brag about. These were the words used when describing the best of the breed, horses like Little Joe and his son Joe Moore; Balleymooney and Red Dog; Zantanon and King; Guinea Pig and Tony; Joe Bailey and Little Joe, Jr.

Today, after a number of years of coupling derogatory adjectives with bulldog or Steel Dust, when the average breeder thinks these words, he pictures a sad horse, round-withered, squatty, overfed, and muscle-bound. The good Steel Dusts were none of these things. There were some poor ones, as in all horses, but on the whole the Quarter Horse was more horse for the height than any other breed in the world.

Major Grove Cullum of the Remount Service was one of the first Thoroughbred enthusiasts to publicly label the Quarter Horse a paragon of faults. He was an excellent horseman and gentleman, but he allowed his love for the Thoroughbred to blind his eyes. He wrote about poor Quarter Horses and good Thoroughbreds. In an article written before the AQHA was organized, he criticized the

101

Quarter Horse for all the faults mentioned above.[3] Since he and others like him were buying horses for the Army Remount Service, it was a most difficult time for the Quarter Horse breeder. Fortunately there were a few independent and hardy ranchers who would not turn their backs on their cherished Steel Dusts in spite of everything the Thoroughbred fans could do or say. These were men such as Billy Anson, Dow Shely, Ott Adams, Coke Roberds, Coke Blake, and Dan Casement.

Dan and Jack Casement came to the defense of the Steel Dust horse. Dan wrote:

> Governmental subsidy of Thoroughbred breeding was all that was needed, virtually to complete the job of weaning the affection of a lot of old-timers from their once cherished "bull-dogs," who had stood by them in sickness and health, labor and levity, and to splice them to a fickle-headed, thinner-thighed equine seductress.[4]

No one has voiced this thought better, before or since.

History has a way of repeating itself, and now, a quarter of a century later, the same thing seems to be happening. The siren song of Thoroughbred blood as a short cut to speed is luring many breeders away from the traditional Quarter Horse. The tendency to use Thoroughbred blood in preference to Quarter Horse blood has increased since the development of organized Quarter racing. When the Quarter Horse Association was organized, the breeders' aim was to perpetuate their cow horse which had a burst of speed when necessary. Few, if any, Quarter Horses were raised with the specific purpose of running. They were run for fun, not as a serious endeavor.

Certainly the quickest way to make a race horse out of the Quarter Horse is to breed to the Thoroughbred. Even better and quicker, buy a couple of sprinting Thoroughbreds. In racing the idea is to get that speed; other considerations seem unimportant. It is this last attitude that has hurt the Quarter Horse. Many ways were found so that sprinting Thoroughbred blood would be registered in the Quarter Horse studbook. One of the most successful

3 "The Western Horse," *Polo*, June, 1935.
4 "Social Significance of the Quarter Horse," *The Cattleman*, September, 1940, 52.

methods was to criticize the old Steel Dust type by saying that the best way to remove his rough spots was to use Thoroughbred blood—breed out weaknesses by crossing. This sounds reasonable —except you are also breeding out type. What, after all said and done, was so wrong with Little Joe, Possum, and their kind? Or for that matter with Red Dog, Joe Moore, or Zantanon? It is true no one would ever take them to be Thoroughbreds. But then they were not.

Another angle was often used when an especially good sprinting Thoroughbred was found, one that produced speed when crossed on Quarter mares. It was pointed out what a great individual he was, how much he had to offer the Quarter Horse, and how seldom such an exception came along. So he and his sons and daughters were registered as exceptional individuals. They were exceptional and wonderful individuals, and they did have a lot to offer the Quarter running horse. They offered speed in exchange for type. In short, the Thoroughbred begot faster sons and daughters, was way up on the list of leading sires of winning horses, and was a better horse for the race track. But he wasn't a Steel Dust. He and his get looked no more like a Steel Dust Quarter Horse than an antelope looks like a mountain lion.

The Quarter Horse has his utility and his typical conformation. He, too, just as the Thoroughbred, has been bred through the years to perform a duty in the most efficient manner. His primary utility is as an all-round utility horse, especially adept at working cattle. As Robert J. Kleberg, Jr., head of the King Ranch in Texas, wrote in 1940—and as subsequently quoted in the *Official Stud Book*:

> He stops and turns easily and does not become leg weary or lazy even when asked to stop and start quickly many times in the course of the day's roping, cutting, or other work.[5]

Dan Casement wrote in the same year:

> The Quarter Horse has no equal in working cattle, the one and

[5] *Official Stud Book and Registry of the American Quarter Horse Association*, I, 1, 10.

only field of equine activity wherein horses are destined never to slump in economic value.[6]

The good Quarter Horse has a terrific burst of speed for a short distance. This speed is needed to catch a calf or turn a steer. Since the love of a horse race is not limited to the Thoroughbred breeder, some Quarter Horses have always been raced, but this is not the reason for their existence or the purpose for which the vast majority were bred. It was an added feature, a built-in bonus, occasionally used. Once in awhile it resulted in fame and publicity. Nowadays many leading breeders make racing and the breeding of race horses the end or goal of their entire breeding program. This is, of course, their right, although it will, if continued, concentrate Thoroughbred blood and result in the loss of the typical conformation of the true Quarter Horse, and the result will be more like a graded Thoroughbred than a great Quarter Horse.

Once again let's listen to Dan Casement. He went right to the heart of the problem of concentrated Thoroughbred blood:

> The prime purpose to which this [the new AQHA] association should aim is the perpetuation of those qualities which are the Quarter Horses' unique and individual traits. To do this successfully requires the scrupulous preservation of the physical characteristics which clearly mark and distinguish this horse from any other breed. Certainly the performance of which he is capable derives directly from his shape. Indeed it has been fashioned purely as a means to an end. If ever the means is corrupted or lost the end will be sacrificed.[7]

Dan Casement then continued saying that the distinctive features of conformation which proclaim the true Steel Dust are his small, sensitive, alert ears, his wise, bright eyes, and the amazing bulk and bulge of his jaw. There is his short back, deep middle and long belly, his low-swung center of gravity, and astonishing expanse of his britches when seen from the rear, surpassing even the width of the croup.

As Bill Anson said, the immense breast and chest, enormous forearm and loin and thigh, and the heavy layers of muscles of the

6 *Ibid.*, 8.   7 *Ibid.*

Quarter Horse are not found in like proportion on any other breed in the world.[8]

As mentioned, racing has traditionally been an avocation or temporary use of the Quarter Horse. However, as parimutuel betting on short races spread throughout the Southwest and West, the demand for racing horses increased until by the late 1950's the most elaborate and expensive breeding programs were aimed at this market. To borrow a phrase from Cunninghame Graham, the racing breeders began to pamper their horses like Christians. This was a far cry from the ranchers' method of turning a stallion and his mares loose in a section or so of hilly and rocky pasture. Horses were hand-bred and carefully nurtured for the race track because that was where the money was. Why worry about the sturdy Steel Dust Quarter Horse with its unique conformation as long as Thoroughbred blood would produce a winner? Someday breeders will be racing only their own kind when all of them take the same route. When that day comes, winners will be harder to produce—and real Quarter Horses hard to find!

If there are those who wish to continue breeding Quarter Horses, they can still do it by selecting the bloodlines they use in their breeding program. A few breeders, especially ranchers, have maintained the integrity of the breed. The old-time Quarter Horse blood should be sought, used, and perpetuated. This way the grandest horse ever to have a saddle cinched on his back will be preserved for posterity.

Let us look at some of the supposed advantages of Thoroughbred blood. One argument used is that the Quarter Horse is just a sprinting Thoroughbred, without benefit of registration. This is not easy to prove wrong. It takes quite a bit of study and historical research before one can appreciate the unique relationship between these two horses. They have been more complementary than competitive down through the years.

Ω Ω Ω Ω CROSSES

The history of the Quarter Horse and the Thoroughbred has been

8 Anson, *Breeding a Rough Country Horse*, 6.

somewhat intermingled since the Thoroughbred became a breed in the early nineteenth century. However, Quarter Horses were popular in the American colonies before this time. What may have been the first Quarter Horse race meet was held at Henrico County, near Petersburg, Virginia, in 1674.[9] This is almost two hundred years before the Thoroughbred's *American Stud Book* was compiled and the first volume issued. Regular races and large purses were common by 1690.

The English Thoroughbred cannot be considered much of a breed before 1729, when his more or less final form and blood was augmented by the importation into England of the Godolphin Barb. If we want to go further and use a strict interpretation of the word breed (as the Thoroughbred breeders like to do when referring to the Quarter Horse), there were no Thoroughbreds until the studbooks were published.

The present *American Stud Book* of the Jockey Club began in the nineteenth century. Nevertheless, the Thoroughbred breeders like to claim every good Quarter Horse as a Thoroughbred, dismissing through ignorance the fact that there were Quarter Horses before there were registered Thoroughbreds or even thoughts of a Thoroughbred studbook—two hundred years before, in fact. These early Quarter Horses were called Quarter Horses—they were raced —their names and pedigrees are well known—and all this prior to the organization of the Thoroughbred owners. When the first Thoroughbreds were selected for entry in an American studbook many Quarter Horses were already registered.

Once registered in a Thoroughbred studbook, the Quarter Horse properly became a Thoroughbred to the Thoroughbred breeder. To the Quarter Horse breeder, he also properly remained a Quarter Horse—heavy set, compact, 14 to 15 hands high, and begetting sprinters, not stayers. Some time the modern Thoroughbred advocates should read the minute descriptions of these early Quarter Horses such as Babraham, Peacock, or Twigg. They were originally recorded as Quarter Horses, and their description will not fit the Thoroughbred, but it will describe the horse that the

9 Herbert, *Frank Forester's Horse and Horsemanship*, I, 130.

AQHA was formed to "collect, record, and preserve." These descriptions are curiously like the "conformation of the Ideal Quarter Horse," as outlined by the founders of the AQHA.

Thoroughbred breeders were looking for stayers, not sprinters. They wanted horses that could run four miles. On the frontier, four-mile races were neither practical nor popular, and the sprinters were hard to find. After Lexington's time,[10] few short-horse breeders bothered to register their horses.

Some Quarter Horses were registered. Those registered, like Peter McCue, never gained any great fame as a Thoroughbred. The frontier Quarter Horse breeder was happy with his sprinter, registered or not. Had he wanted a long horse he could have found him in the likes of Glencoe, American Eclipse, Lexington, Diomed, or Boston. They were the greyhounds of the turf, but they were not what the short-horse man wanted. He was bulldog searching.

When superior performance is claimed for animals having an infusion of Thoroughbred blood, the type of performance usually mentioned is racing. Therefore most breeders should accept this argument with caution. They know that sustained speed, on beautifully smooth, artificial footing, is not comparable to running down a steer over the rocky and rough land found on a cattle range, nor is it a pleasant gallop over a mountain meadow or where there is downed timber. Can running with a total weight of 110 pounds be compared with a cutting horse performing under 250 pounds of man and saddle? There is, to put it bluntly, performance and performance. What type of performance do you look for in a Quarter Horse? He should have a quick burst of speed, ability to duck, dodge, and turn while running at full speed, the ability to stay on his feet when the going gets rugged, and the ability to carry a full-sized man all day without tiring. That kind of performance you find in the Steel Dust, not in the Thoroughbred.

It is true that some top breeders, present and past, use or used Thoroughbred blood. You never read about all of those who used

---

[10] Lexington was foaled in 1851. He began racing as a three-year-old and soon was considered the greatest distance horse of his time.

it and failed. No really outstanding breeder has ever been able to use it successfully for more than one or two generations—and then only with an exceptional horse. We cannot all breed to these exceptions. Among the greatest breeders of the last one hundred years, such men as Bill Fleming, Crawford Sykes, Bill Anson, Coke Roberds, Ott Adams, Coke Blake, Dan Casement, and others of their caliber, any Thoroughbred blood they used was entirely incidental. They did not believe in using it except for just cause and with due care. The same is true today among the real Quarter Horse breeders. One of the greatest reasons for their success is the purity of their horses. They produce Quarter Horses capable of doing it all—all a Quarter Horse should do. In short, it is not true that all great breeders, past and present, used Thoroughbred blood. They used it only when the Thoroughbred was also a Quarter Horse, and when that horse offered the breeder some Quarter Horse characteristic he needed in his stock.

8. PERFORMANCE

THE BACKGROUND of the Quarter Horse eminently fitted him for the new life he was to lead when he left the Atlantic Coast. His evolution had been guided by a people who lived a rough and rural life and in whose hard work and rough play he had always been a favorite figure. Now the descendants of these men and their Quarter Horses moved into an environment for which they seemed to be endowed by nature. It was to the cattle country of the American West, where the Quarter Horse was to blossom and to find a new life and the belated recognition that his worth demanded.

The modern Quarter Horse has been bred largely on the range alongside cattle. Here racing was always secondary, but this latent ability was never forgotten by his owners. Therefore, it is only natural that the Quarter Horse should be a master of two trades—cattle and short racing. In the years before the 1860's when he specialized in quick speed, the Quarter Horse was a thing of beauty mighty pleasing to the cowman. Every contour of his body reflected the purpose for which he was bred. The cowman made a cow horse out of the sprinter. In fact, the cow horse became so accustomed to working with stock that by 1940 even a green Quarter colt in the presence of cattle would be stimulated to do what was expected of him as if by conditioned response.

The conformation of the Quarter Horse is his greatest asset in working cattle, just as it is in short racing. His chunky build makes him the stoutest on the end of a rope, the handiest on which to cut a herd, and the fastest and safest when keeping a wild one from reaching the brush. He is perhaps the only horse in America with a strictly economic future. Trucks and cars have completely replaced the roadster and the draft horse but not the stock horse.

Ω Ω Ω Ω RANCH AND RODEO

With a few exceptions, all of the great ranch and rodeo horses are Quarter Horses. Since ranch horses do not normally appear in competition, the relative merits of the outstanding horses are difficult to compare. Rodeo horses and race horses, on the other hand, can be compared, and the outstanding horses can be selected more easily.

When the branding chute appeared, near the end of the nineteenth century, the old-timers figured that great cow horses and roping horses would soon become a thing of the past. Perhaps their numbers diminished somewhat, but they were still necessary. A new institution appeared at almost the same time—the rodeo. Any top horses that were not needed on the ranches were now in demand for the rodeo. The rodeo was to become the proving ground for man and horse. Some of the greatest cowboys and cow horses of all times were to appear in the competitions. Cowboys developed greater speed, accuracy, and all-round ability than their predecessors who worked part time and without prize money to spur them on to beat the next contestant.

The rodeo has developed into one of the great American sports, and the rodeo rider today is a popular figure. But without the help of a horse, no calf roper can tie his animal in money time, no steer roper can hope to succeed, no bulldogger can expect a purse, no cow-milker can hope to place, no team ropers can win, no cutting horse rider can reach the finals. Rhythmic co-operation between horse and rider is essential. Both must do their part, and neither can succeed without the other.

Most of the top horses on the rodeo circuit carry Quarter Horse blood. There have been exceptional horses of other breeds which were good, but the simple answer lies in the fact that most other breeds do not have what it takes for ranch and rodeo work. They were bred for draft work, pleasure riding, trotting, long-distance racing, or some other feature. Only the Quarter Horse has been

110

bred for those two things which every cow horse and every rodeo horse must have to be worthy of the name—a cool head and rapid breaking speed. The ability to stand quiet and flatfooted one moment and to be running at full speed the next is a prerequisite.

All cow horses and rodeo horses must be carefully trained for their work. Steer-roping horses are taught to run on after the catch and, when the steer is down, to face away from the animal to be tied. The calf horse must be taught to stop when the loop is thrown and to face the calf. All roping horses must be taught to keep a tight rope. The dogging horse must be taught to catch and run beside the steer, and when his rider leaves him, to wait and see if his rider needs to try again. If his rider does want to jump again, he must stand quietly while his owner runs up to him. The horse which hazes for the bulldogger must be taught not to run past the steer, to stop when the steer stops, etc. Team roping horses must be taught to work as a team and to work on either the head or the hind feet. A cutting horse has to learn so much that in the range country men are still arguing whether one is born or trained. There is one quality which the Quarter Horse possesses which each and every one of these horses must have above all others—quick maneuverable speed, the ability to start and gain full speed in the shortest possible time. They also must have the temperament to stand quietly at all times.

The ability to remain quiet under stress is often referred to as levelheadedness. Levelheadedness, quietness even after strenuous action, is a priceless attribute enjoyed by all properly trained Quarter Horses. It is a factor which is too often ignored. One of the greatest, if not the greatest, dogging horses of all time, Mike Hastings' Stranger, had this quality to a marked degree. He would stand in the chute with his breast against the barrier, quivering with excitement, while waiting for the starting signal. He almost never broke the barrier before the flag unless the flagman made some unusual or sudden movement. Hog-Eye, the horse that Roy Adams trained and sold to Bob Crosby, was another outstanding horse which was always cool headed and alert. Colonel Clyde, ridden by John Bowman, and Mark, ridden by Carl Arnold, are two more.

111

Rodeo horses and cow horses must repeat their work time and time again each afternoon and not get excited. In addition to the ability to gain momentum rapidly, probably the Quarter Horse's greatest asset is his levelheadedness and quiet temper.

Rodeo work is not work for a soft horse which must be pampered. To begin with, the horse must carry around two hundred pounds when working and running his best. Then, during the strenuous competition, he does not always receive considerate treatment because the rider is working against time, and cannot be concentrating on the horse. After the horse has been worked hard all afternoon, later that same day he may be loaded into a trailer (where he cannot lie down or even go to sleep on his feet because of constant movement) and be driven four or five hundred miles to another contest.

Between 1900 and 1940 any number of great horses have worked in rodeo arenas. Joe Gardner's horse, Rowdy, used by Joe and Clay McGonigal, was tops. He carried Clay to the international steer-roping championship in 1907. Clay made a record on him in seventeen and two-fifths seconds, which stood for a long, long time. Rowdy was a Billy Quarter Horse and was some horse. Dusty, owned by Milt Good, was also quite a horse. Roamer, owned by Billy Bonnell, was used for exhibition steer roping when his front legs were hobbled. Ellison Carroll, Fred Beason, Buffalo Vernon, and even Lucille Mulhall rode Roamer at various times.

Roy Adams claimed Silver was the greatest roping horse he ever saw in action. Jake McClure roped and tied five calves on him in eighty-two seconds one year in Denver. This is a sixteen and two-thirds average. Silver was a sorrel gelding, and he received the Prince of Wales trophy for being the best working rodeo horse. Jake did his best roping and won most of his money on Silver. Legs, another of McClure's horses, was everyone's pet.

Several other outstanding horses must be mentioned. Comet, Bob Crosby's horse, was also one of the all-time greats, as was his June Bug. Honey Boy, a roping horse owned by Juan Salinas, carried Toots Mansfield to world championship honors. He was a Cotton Eyed Joe colt raised by George Clegg. Jake McClure won

112

a calf roping at Madison Square Garden on Honey Boy. Bartender carried Clyde Burke to similar honors. Baldy, another Burke horse, originally owned by Ike Rude, was even better. On Baldy, Burke won the Madison Square Garden and Cheyenne shows in the same year. After Burke's untimely death, Troy Fort rode Baldy to even greater honors. Baldy was raised by John Dawson and was by Old Red Buck. Brown Waggoner, a Three D horse, was one of the greatest dogging horses of 1939. In 1940, Red, Dog Town Slim's horse, had this honor. Speaking of dogging horses, Stranger, Mike Hastings' red roan, is generally considered the greatest that ever lived. It took a real rider to stay aboard him when he broke from the barrier. In one year Stranger carried riders in ninety-two contests and won ninety first moneys and two seconds. Coon Dog, owned by Dog Town Slim, was a Sam Watkins gelding raised by George Clegg, of Alice, Texas. He also was a top bulldogging horse.

Bullet was another great roping horse. He was ridden by such riders as Ike Rude, John Bowman, Everett Shaw, and King Merritt. In 1941 Ike Rude won the world's champion RCA steer-roping title on his back. In 1942, King Merritt won the same title on him. Bullet was sired by Jack McCue. Hoyt Lewis raised him and Bob Crosby trained him.[1]

A list of the great cow horses and rodeo horses reads like a list of Who's Who in the Quarter Horse world, and that is pretty close to what it is, because that is why they were bred—for ranch and rodeo purposes.

Rodeo and racing are contests, and more often than not there is considerable money for the winner. The working cow horse must earn his keep in a more utilitarian fashion. Regardless of how good a Quarter Horse may be on a ranch, his fame is only local.

---

[1] For those interested in rodeo horses, perhaps the best single source is the fine magazine of rodeo entitled *Hoofs and Horns*. It is edited by Willard H. Porter, one-time editor of *Quarter Horse Journal*, and horseman who used to be a pretty fair roper himself. Incidentally, Porter has written many fine articles about horses and ropers. Another source of rodeo information is Jerry Armstrong's column in *The Western Horseman*. This column began back in the 1930's and was originally entitled "The Collegiate Cowboy's Column." When the magazine changed editors in the mid-forties, it became "Picked Up in the Rodeo Arena," and it still goes by that title. The column is full of information about horses and their riders.

The breeding establishments one finds today, where the production of Quarter Horses is a separate business, is something new, brought on by the sudden demand for Quarter Horses. This is the way it was, before the long-horse became popular, when all production was aimed at producing a sprinter. Later, when the four-mile race became fashionable nobody but the western farmers and ranchers wanted a Quarter Horse. These men knew good horse-flesh, and the qualities of the Quarter Horse, especially his disposition and his short speed, fitted their requirements. There was occasionally a market for a fast horse or a polo prospect, but the rancher did not breed with this in mind because the market was too small. He bred for his own use.

On the western ranch there always seemed to be too much work and too few men. A *remuda* of top horses could be found on the successful ranch because good horses saved time and allowed each man to do his work faster and more efficiently. Good Quarter Horses sired most of the cow horses, although many of the dams were just ordinary mares. The western rancher bought the best Quarter Horse stallion he could find. Then by keeping his top mares to breed and occasionally changing stallions, he was able to improve his horses.

Times have not changed too much today. The modern cattle ranch that is making money still has top horses. Today, however, the Quarter Horses are loaded into a truck or trailer and driven to the area where the cattle are to be worked. After the work is done, they are reloaded and returned to headquarters. Hours of riding to the job and back are thus eliminated. Top racing or polo prospects are still sold, and some ranches, such as the King Ranch, hold regular Quarter Horse sales.

The horse is still indispensable on the large western ranch. As civilization expands onto the flat lands, the cattle ranch is pushed farther back into the rough country. How, except on horseback, can you bring the cattle to the roundup; how, except on horseback, can you go into a spooky herd and bring out the animal you want? Endless jobs to be done by a cattle outfit cry for horses—always have and always will.

114

LEO, BY JOE REED II

JOE BAILEY OF GONZALES (*above*)

PHOTO BY ROBERT M. DENHARDT

JOE HANCOCK, BY JOHN WILKINS

PHOTO BY ROBERT M. DENHARDT

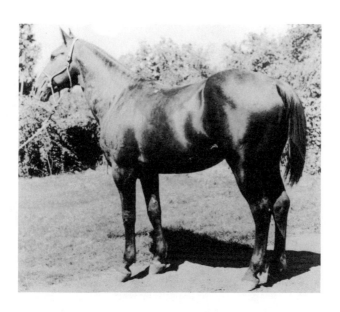

MARK, BY RED CLOUD BY POSSUM (*above*)
Great sire of roping, rodeo, and cow horses.

MIDNIGHT, BY BADGER BY PETER MCCUE
The Waggoner D may be seen on his shoulder.

BALLEYMOONEY (*above*)
Dan Casement's great stallion by Concho Colonel
by Anson's Jim Ned.

ZANTANON
As a five-year-old, after defeating Conesa in Mexico.

My Texas Dandy (*above*)
Sire of Clabber, Colonel Clyde, and other
fast Quarter Horses.

Clabber
Sire of fast Quarter Horses in Arizona and California.

FLYING BOB (*above*)
A great Louisiana race horse, whose sire was Chicaro.

UNCLE JIMMY GRAY
Sired by the Thoroughbred Bonnie Joe by Faustus.

THE OLD SORREL (*above*)
Foundation sire of King Ranch Quarter Horses, by Hickory Bill.

OLD JOE REED
Son of Joe Blair and Della Moore.

PLAUDIT
Reflects glory to the Quarter Horse and Palomino. Sire of some of the
fastest and most beautiful horses in the Rocky Mountain region.

Ω Ω Ω Ω EARLY SHORT RACING

Short races have been popular in America ever since the colonies were settled. Quarter racing in America has not been, in spite of its popularity, well organized until recently. A great deal of confusion arose not only over what was proper or improper but also concerning records of time and the pedigrees of the horses. It was not until the establishment of several organizations, beginning in 1940 (all of which eventually were absorbed by the AQHA), that any order began to appear.

There never has been a time when short races were not held some place in America. By 1700 there were large purses being offered along the Atlantic seacoast. Most of these races were matches between local champions. As mentioned previously, the first reference to a short race I have encountered was one held in Henrico County, Virginia, in 1674, 130 years before the first recorded meet for long horses.

Short racing disappeared first near the metropolitan centers, remained longest in the rural areas, and moved gradually westward across the country with the frontier. It seems to have followed the rural zone immediately behind the frontier. Perhaps this is because the Quarter Horse has always been the common man's horse, a utility animal; at home he could help put in a crop or herd cattle; in front of a buggy or buckboard he could go to church, a camp meeting, or even to a race. He was normally owner-raised, owner-trained, owner-worked, and owner-raced.

Kentucky, Missouri, Illinois, and Tennessee were settled as America moved westward. For the first time all horses were American bred and raised. Great care was taken in selecting stallions, since most of the long horses, capable of running four-mile races, were not satisfactory Quarter Horse sires. The most popular sires were descendants of Janus, Brimmer, Timoleon, and Sir Archy. Also present at the time were some new bloodlines, namely, stallions sired by Kentucky Whip, Baccus, Printer, and Copperbottom.

The last half of the nineteenth century provided more than its share of famous race horse sires. Good examples are Shiloh, Steel Dust, Billy, Cold Deck, and Rondo. These were the first stallions

115

to which modern short-races can trace their ancestry with any accuracy. By 1900 the immediate predecessors of the modern racing Quarter Horse appeared. This group included such notables as Peter McCue, Traveler, Rondo, Hickory Bill, and Joe Bailey.

One of the least important factors in short racing had been the track. Any opening, fairly straight, could do for a race track. On the frontier the length of the race would often be determined by the room needed to pull up in after the finish line was crossed. There are many records of jockeys' being brushed off by tree limbs or getting thrown into a creek before they could stop their mounts after a race. Even a Quarter Horse would prefer one hundred yards to slow down in after a race, but often had to settle for fifty or less. In brushy or wooded country the main street of a town often furnished the best track on which to hold a race. If the race was in the prairie country, making a track was a simple proposition. Interested persons would make two parallel paths by dragging a heavy article. Then each horse would have his own path on which to run.

In the early 1900's more attention was paid to the tracks. Oval tracks appeared at most county fairgrounds, and any small town might have a straightaway of around three-eighths mile. Generally, the finish line was marked with stakes at every common distance, 110, 220, 300, 330, 400, and 440 yards. In the beginning there were no stalls for starting, and starts were made by the "lap-and-tap" or "ask-and-answer" systems. In a short race the start was so important that every effort was made to find some way to see that the other horse did not get an advantage.

In the lap-and-tap, the horses were ridden slowly up to the line, and if they were both moving, and closely lapped, they were tapped off by the starter. Each jockey of course wanted to be ahead, and if he was not, he would pull up so that the horses would not be lapped, then the start was off. A great deal of time was often spent before the race was started and a nervous, excitable horse was not often the winner. The Quarter Horse had an advantage with his quiet disposition.

The ask-and-answer system was somewhat similar except that

116

the jockeys started themselves. If one was ready, he would say, "Ready." If the other jockey and his horse were ready, he would answer, "Ho," and the race was on. If he did not answer immediately, then that opportunity was lost and one or the other would have to say "ready" again when he was satisfied. This method could be used in open chutes, on the line, or with "walk-ups." In the last type of start, both horses were supposed to walk up to the starting line the same as in a lap-and-tap.

There were many abuses, since each owner and jockey tried for the advantage. The sharpest man or the quietest horse had all the odds in his favor. The owner of the quietest horse could spoil several starts until the other horse became nervous, flighty, and tired. Sometimes it took hours or even days to get a really big match race off the mark.

Since the horse was often worked as well as raced, the owner was generally not a professional, nor did he need to be. Expensive equipment and professional help were not needed for the short races because training, although helpful, was not as important in a short race as in a long one. But by the same token, the nonprofessional was often an easy mark for a sharp race horse operator. When a couple of well-known horses were matched, people came from miles around. The occasion was generally taken as a holiday, and it brought out people from all walks of life. Ranchers, farmers, city sports, cowboys, Mexicans, Indians, and new immigrants, all lined up side by side to watch and bet on the race.

Since there were no rules, except as might be arranged for that particular match, extensive dickering went on as each side tried to get the advantage or tried not to be at a disadvantage. Conditions for a race almost always included when and where the race was to be run, who were to be starters and who finish judges, how far the race was to be run, and the weight to be carried by each horse. Occasionally, seemingly unimportant factors, such as when the horses should arrive on the track, how the track was to be prepared, what the jockeys could carry on the horse,[2] whether separate lanes

2 What the jockey would be allowed to carry on the horse could be more important than it might seem to the casual observer, for example, a battery that would give a

117

were to be used, how much forfeit money must be posted, under what circumstances, such as a muddy track, one could refuse the start, and who decided if the track was muddy, all such problems led to endless discussion. When two really top horses met, these factors were not too important, but second-rate and third-rate horses needed all the breaks, and when owned by a person whose first interest was money and not whether or not he had the faster horse, the setting of conditions could be a long-drawn-out process. One of the weirdest races run was when two owners who wanted to find out who had the faster horse but who were afraid the other would get the advantage tried to match a race. They ended up swapping jockeys and betting on the jockeys.

One of the first attempts to organize short racing was the Quarter Horse Camp Meeting Association, composed for the most part of the men who created the AQHA who liked to race. After one year's operation the name was changed to the Quarter Horse Race Meeting Association of America. This action was taken because a majority of the "Stud Horse Cavaliers," as the members called themselves, felt that "Camp Meeting" did not properly describe their activities. They intended to sponsor Quarter Horse meets on a nonprofessional and nonprofit basis. Ideally the members were to raise, train, and race their own horses. Let me quote from the official information bulletin of the association.

> Standards have been enacted under which the Quarter Running Horse may be tested and judged on the "Quarter Paths." The Race Meeting Ass'n has opened a Quarter Running Horse Register for the purpose of permanently recording the records, descriptions and pedigrees of celebrated Quarter Running Horses. Horses entered in the Register will receive a certificate, and will bear the title "Qualified Quarter Running Horse."[3]

shock when applied to a sweaty neck, or even an innocent looking few links of chain. When a horse was properly "conditioned" in his stall, just the rattle of a few links could, through fear, put wings on his feet.

[3] This is from the mimeographed newsletter entitled *The Quarter Horse, Voice of the Quarter Horse Race Meeting Association of America*, No. 4, March, 1942. Only about half a dozen of these newsletters were ever distributed; they were compiled by Jim Hall, first treasurer of the AQHA. He also was the instigator of that exclusive organization known as "Stud Horse Cavaliers." *Denhardt Files*, Quarter Racing Folder, 4.

This group stated that Quarter Horse conformation was an absolute must for entry into their racing record book and felt the association's activities would act as a "feeder" to the AQHA *Stud Book*. They said that both associations would co-operate for the good and betterment of the American Quarter Horse. In order for a horse to obtain registration, it was required that speed testing be accomplished under electrically timed, photo finish conditions, and that the application show the horse's pedigree and conformation. Jim Hall was president, George Clegg, Raymond Dickson, and Jim Minnick were vice-presidents, and Jess York, treasurer. Although the bulletins stated that "The directors included prominent Quarter Horse Breeders throughout the United States," only three were mentioned, D. W. Williams, Helen Michaelis, and W. H. George. The records show that this organization was connected with only two race meets, held in Eagle Pass, Texas, one in October, 1941, and one in April, 1942. Both of these meets were first-rate, and the moving force behind them was Helen Michaelis.

Ω Ω Ω Ω ORGANIZED SHORT RACING

The racing organization which was to be the most successful was Melville Haskell's Tucson group. Before 1945, it was primarily a local activity of the horsemen in that area. While Melville had a lot of good help, he was the one who saw that everything was ready at the Hacienda Moltacqua Track in Tucson, where the first meets were held. Other men who were active included Bob Locke, Rukin Jelks, Jake Meyer, Clancy Wollard, and Joe Flieger. A new track was built at Rillito, Arizona, after a few years, and during the winter of 1943–44 the racing group put on 125 races at the new track for Quarter Horses. After the move to Rillito, Melville had the dual jobs of acting as presiding steward and handicapper.

Brand new regulations had to be created to cover this new kind of race meet, where the owner was generally the trainer and the horse his favorite riding animal. The rules were a rather curious amalgamation of Thoroughbred race rules, match race traditions, and on-the-spot innovations. To begin with, the old-faithful Thoroughbred method of handicapping by having a claiming race

119

wouldn't work. Under that system, if a horse was entered in a $500 claiming race, anybody could post $500 and claim any horse in the race by naming him in writing prior to post time. Because the Quarter Horse generally had a cow horse value (as a stud, or cutting horse, or roping horse, for example) greater than his racing abilities, claiming did not work. Even if the horse couldn't race, the owner still wanted to keep him.

Mel Haskell worked out the handicapping by establishing a sort of dual system, one for the better horse and one for the "run for fun" boys. The horses were classified A, B, C, and D. Class A and B had weight handicaps and C and D were generally run with weight allowances for age and sex. Generally speaking, an A or B horse could run in twenty-four seconds or under while C and D horses would run the quarter mile in twenty-four seconds or over. Each time the horses ran, their times were kept and their abilities charted. The slowest B horses carried 110 pounds, and weight was then added, 15 pounds for each one-fifth second to 200 pounds for the top of A. Actually no horse carried more than 135 very often. If too good a horse tried to get in a race, the weight he had to carry made winning almost impossible, and a poor horse couldn't win because there were no jockeys light enough to give him the necessary advantage. Horses were reclassified after each meeting and moved up or down according to their apparent class. Unknown horses started at the top in order to be classified. Haskell also had friends at other short race meets, held at King City and Corona, California, Reno, Nevada, and at Eagle Pass and Del Rio, Texas. They would exchange times and other information so that any horses showing up at one of the tracks would be known. This way they were all protected, and the system also led to the formation of a racing organization to cover the southern and western states.

During the first few years there were really only two top-notch horses, Clabber and Shue Fly. Clabber was the old iron horse owned by A. A. Nichols of Gilbert, Arizona, who was discussed earlier. He was the first to come on the scene. The next horse was Shue Fly, the mare owned by Elmer and Charlie Hepler of Carlsbad, New Mexico. She was sired by Cowboy who was by Yellow Jacket and out of Roan Lady by Stalks by John Wilkins. Shue Fly was making a name for herself in Colorado and New Mexico when the Heplers decided she might be the horse to beat Clabber. In December, 1941, they moved her to Arizona. The climate was right, nobody in Arizona thought Clabber could be beaten. They did not believe it even when it happened. Shue Fly was rematched again against Clabber to run 440 yards on December 7, 1941, this time in Tucson, a day many Arizonans were to remember for two reasons. Here is what one of the "New Believers," Joe Flieger, had to say about it:

> Not being an old timer I can't testify about the greatness of earlier Quarter Horses, but I will, if I live long enough, be able to tell a great deal about what I believe to be the greatest Quarter Horse that ever stuck a nose under a wire.
>
> I am referring to Shue Fly. Now I had to see this mare run to believe that any horse could come from behind and catch Clabber. Well I, and some of my friends, found out the hard way by losing several dollars on a match race at Phoenix. Not being satisfied we tried again. That made a believer out of me. I do know I can in future years when there are new champions running, rear back and say, "Well men, I know your horses are good, but boy, did you ever see Shue Fly fly?"[4]

Shue Fly was a dark sorrel, with a long star and a white fetlock. She also had a distinguishing white mark between her girth and flank. Like many running Quarter Horses, she was not as compact as the ideal Quarter Horse should be.

The first race Shue Fly ran was probably the race in Trinidad in 1940. In this race she ran with two other horses the distance, one-half mile. The famous Question Mark beat her, but it was his last race because he broke down at the end and finished on three legs. At that time Shue Fly was trained and owned by Bob Burris.

Shue Fly was champion in 1942, 1943, and 1944. She had competition in Nobody's Friend, Clabber, Red Man, and Rosita, but

4 Joe Flieger, "Shue Fly, the Greatest Quarter Horse," *The Western Horseman,* June, 1944, 18.

121

she beat them all when the chips were down. In 1945 when Shue Fly was sick, Queenie won the championship race, but Squaw H and Dee Dee both had beaten her in important races and she was not considered the world's champion. Champion stallions in the early years were Clabber, in 1941, and Nobody's Friend, in 1942. Nobody's Friend finished a nose behind Shue Fly and ahead of Clabber, setting a new stallion record of twenty-two and seven-tenths seconds. Joe Reed was a champion stallion in 1943, beating Clabber and Chicaro for the honors. In 1944, Piggin String and Texas Lad were the main contenders, but since they did not meet, neither received the honor. Dee Dee won the championship in 1945 by beating Queenie, Piggin String, and Jeep B. In 1946, Queenie was named World's Champion Quarter Horse. At this time, how-ever, a new star who was to outshine Clabber, Shue Fly, and Queenie, Miss Princess, was appearing on the horizon. Miss Prin-cess was a King Ranch Thoroughbred, raced by Ernest Lane. She was by Bold Venture out of Bruja by Livery.[5]

Miss Princess went to Del Rio, Texas, in 1946 for the annual race meet. Here she found little competition. On May 17 she beat Vandy and Wee Tot, running an easy 440 yards in twenty-two and four-tenths seconds. Miss Princess returned to Del Rio for the October meet, and here she proved beyond doubt that she was made of championship material. Before a record-breaking crowd she gave a preview of what she was to do the following year to Shue Fly. The feature race of that meet was named in honor of General Wainwright, who was on hand to see it run. Entered were Miss Princess, Blondie, a stout-hearted daughter of a great sire,

---

[5] So popular did the races in Tucson become that the group soon had to put out a racing form, or chart. It started as a resumé of the year's activities and was first pub-lished in 1943, compiled and edited by Melville H. Haskell. The second came out in 1944. Both appeared under the name *Racing Quarter Horses*, sponsored by the Southern Arizona Horse Breeders Association. The next year, 1945, the annual record was called *The Quarter Running Horse*, and it was published by the newly organized American Quarter Racing Association. Thereafter it was published regularly until the racing group was absorbed by the AQHA in 1950. The various early booklets and mimeo-graphed leaflets put out by the officials running these early Quarter Horse meets are invaluable. They list horses running, how they were classified, records made, statistics, racing charts and forms, applications for member tracks, confidential blacklists and penalties imposed, pictures, and much else of value. See *Denhardt Files*, Quarter Racing Folders 1–5.

Jimmie Alred, Danger Boy, a brilliant young stallion owned by George Parr, and Mae West. In this race you could have covered the three mares and a stallion with a blanket, but Miss Princess had what it takes to bring home $11,000.

Several days after this race Miss Princess was taken to Eagle Pass, for her last meet of 1946. Here she won the open 330-yard race when she equaled the world's record of seventeen and four-tenths seconds. On the last day of the meet she won the Eagle Pass Derby of 440 yards in twenty-two and five-tenths seconds. All in all, it was a satisfactory year for Bob Kleberg, Ernest Lane, and Miss Princess. Her half brother, Assault, was also showing real promise.

The hour which Bob Kleberg and Ernest Lane had been waiting for came almost sooner than they expected. Elmer Hepler never was one to avoid a good race, and with Shue Fly he did not have to. To be brief, Shue Fly came to Del Rio in May, 1947, to see what all the talk was about this Miss Princess, and a race was promptly matched.

The stands were packed to overflowing and a purse of $30,000 awaited the winner. May 4 was the day. The horses went to the gate promptly, and for the first time the Del Rio track was laned so that each mare would have a fair run without interference. Shue Fly was exercised more than Miss Princess, and Shue Fly cut up badly in the gate delaying the start almost half an hour. When the gate was finally sprung, Miss Princess made her bid and the race was no longer a question. Shue Fly, always a great mare, ran the 440 in a little better than twenty-two and five-tenths, fast enough to beat almost any other horse, but not fast enough for Miss Princess, who ran it that day in world's record time, twenty-two and three-tenths seconds, for the standing start quarter. Pat Castile, who rode Miss Princess, said that the race never gave him a worry after they broke. Both he and Earl Southern, who rode Shue Fly, weighed in at 111 pounds. Bob Kleberg came to see that race even though he had to miss Assault's winning of Jamaica's Grey Lag Stakes to do it. Wild horses could not have kept that Texan away when this race was run.

123

There were other outstanding horses running at the same time as Miss Princess, and, had she not appeared, they might well have been more famous. These include such horses as Miss Bank, Lightfoot, Jimmy, Hyglo, B Seven, Blondie L, Hard Twist, Miss Panama, Stella Moore, and Leota W, just to mention a few.

By 1946 the work of keeping records for the rapidly expanding short-racing industry demanded a more representative organization, so Melville Haskell called a meeting, and the American Quarter Racing Association was organized on February 1, 1945.[6]

As vice-president of the AQHA, Bob Denhardt became the official representative of the AQHA on the racing association board of directors. Other directors of the racing association were also directors of the AQHA, among them Melville Haskell, Helen Michaelis, Bill Lamkin, Elmer Hepler, and Jack Casement. The idea of the new organization was to get better representation for the short tracks that were gaining momentum throughout the Southwest from Texas to California. The AQRA grew rapidly on the solid foundation Melville Haskell had built. By 1949, several states had legalized parimutuel betting on Quarter Horses. Consequently state racing commissions had to have an organization to turn to for positive identification. Some states put the burden of proof on the AQHA, others on the AQRA. Since the AQHA was not at the time equipped to do this work and since there were two other organizations available, something had to be done. There just could not be an AQHA, an AQRA, and a NQHBA and have successful short racing. Haskell took the necessary steps. First he got in touch with Joe Huffington, prominent in the NQHBA, and Bob Hooper, president of the AQHA. He could speak for the AQHA himself. After a series of meetings he convinced everyone of the necessity for consolidation, and the NQHBA and the AQRA joined the AQHA; since then there has been only one group. Quarter racing now entered its modern active period. A somewhat disorganized beginning had blossomed into a great modern sport.

[6] This meeting was held in the picturesque Old Pueblo Club in Tucson. Most of the Southwestern states, as well as Florida, were represented. It was decided that all racing Quarter Horses would be given a certificate, which would give the owner a membership and vote in the organization.

9. EARLY BREEDERS

I T WAS MY GOOD FORTUNE to have known and talked with all but one of the following breeders, the exception being William Anson. I was able to visit the ranch and examine Anson's records and talk with Mrs. Anson. Dan Casement was more than a casual acquaintance, and I had the privilege of spending days as his guest, both at his home in Manhattan and at the Denver stock shows. In many ways Dan D. Casement was the greatest American I have ever met, or ever expect to meet.

The accounts of these early breeders are a composite of what the breeders themselves said and in some cases wrote, and material gathered from other sources. There are inconsistencies, and they are unavoidable. This is because when two authorities disagree, often there is no longer any way to check the information. If some of these men have erred, they should be allowed some leeway on dates, figures, and names when recalling what happened fifty years before. Most accurate are the Anson and Casement stories because these men wrote about their horses many years ago when the details were still fresh.

COKE BLAKE (1862)

PEGGS, OKLAHOMA
Sept. 30, 1916

TO WHOM IT MAY CONCERN:

This is to certify that I know the Alsup people and their white Lightening horses, having raced with them for several years. They were among the very best of horses. I have trained and tried Tu-bal-cain, the Blake Horse, and believe him to be the most

125

valuable horse I ever knew. He is the fastest horse I ever handled and very sensible. I have seen the Blake herd of horses; they are an improvement over Cold Deck and White Lightenings.

SMALL BAKER[1]

The letter by Small Baker quoted above is a good introduction to Blake and his horses. Coke Blake produced a family of powerfully muscled horses by crossing the Bertrands, the Brimmers, the White Lightnings, and the Cold Decks.

The Bertrands were a very popular family line and references can be found to them in all of the early studbooks. The first of the line was foaled in 1821 and was sired by Sir Archy by imported Diomed. According to Wallace in his *American Stud-Book,* Sir Archy's best son was Bertrand, who was as good on the turf as he was in the stud. Wallace relates that his blood was sought in all western pedigrees and that he improved the stock of both Kentucky and Tennessee. Bertrand had several sons and grandsons named after him. He ended his life in the ownership of Lindsey and Hutchcraft in Kentucky, dying in the spring of 1838. Sons of Bertrand who carried his name were owned by Henry Shacklet of Virginia, John M. Ginnis of Pennsylvania, Alfred King of Kentucky, and James Richardson of South Carolina. In this fashion his blood was widely scattered and the popularity of the family increased.[2]

The Brimmers were a similar family of heavily muscled shorthorses. Here again the historian runs into problems as Edgar lists eight, Wallace six, and Bruce eight. Bruce enters all he lists in the Appendix, showing that he considers them less than thoroughly bred. Most of the early Brimmers lived in Virginia, Kentucky, or

---

[1] This quotation is by a well-known race horse personality, Small Baker, and is one of the dozen or so testimonials found in the interesting little booklet entitled *The Pride of Mayes County.* No author is given, but when Blake presented a copy to me, he said he had prepared it himself and that it was the first book written about Quarter Horses. It was privately printed by the Republican Printery of Pryor, Oklahoma. It is eight pages, bound in brown paper which looks like leather, and is 3¾x7¼ inches. There is no date given, but a good estimate would be 1923. The only other items written by Coke Blake that I know of are, first, a recollection of his early days which appeared in *Ranchman,* November, 1948, under the heading "Steel Dust . . ."; and secondly, a few paragraphs ascribed to him appearing in the same magazine in April, 1943, under the title, "If He Is a Good Horse Listen for the Roar of Distant Thunder."

[2] Wallace, *American Stud-Book,* 61.

126

South Carolina. The original Brimmer belonged to John Goode of Powhatan County, Virginia, and Bruce lists him as being by Herod, although Will Williams, writing from Popular Grove, Tennessee, on March 25, 1856, says that Eclipse was the sire of Brimmer and that his father owned Eclipse.[3] In any case, there was a Brimmer horse in Tennessee from which Blake obtained his infusion of Brimmer blood.

The White Lightnings, according to Blake, were known as the Alsup horses, after Shelp Alsup, who was a breeder of fast short-horses in Tennessee and Missouri after the Civil War. According to Blake, they were for the most part about 15 hands high, steel gray in color, and weighed in the neighborhood of 1,300 pounds. Young White Lightnings were supposed to be the fastest 300-yard horses in existence at that time.

The last founder of one of the four families of horses crossed by Coke Blake was Cold Deck, who is taken up elsewhere in this book. However, to quote Coke Blake again, Cold Deck was the admiration of all who knew him on account of his beauty, style, speed, and intelligence.

Samuel Coke Blake was born near Cane Hill, Arkansas, on April 10, 1862. His mother was a native of Arkansas, but his father was a school teacher who came to America from England in 1840. Blake's first horse was a Steel Dust mare given to him by his uncle, Samuel Murray, who bought the mare in Bonham, Texas. When Coke was twenty, he left Arkansas and worked on the railroad in Colorado for a time. Later he worked for a cousin who had a flour mill at Tahlequah in the Cherokee Nation. As soon as he had saved a little money, he bought some cattle and began ranching near Pryor, Oklahoma, which then was also in the Cherokee Nation. In 1888 he married a Cherokee woman who bore him three sons and six daughters.

In 1896, Napoleon Bonaparte Maxwell came to the Blake ranch riding a striking bay gelding sired by Cold Deck. He had bought the horse while he lived in Wendell, Tennessee. Coke had seen Old Cold Deck at Van Buren some years before, and he knew Foster

[3] Herbert, *Frank Forester's Horse and Horsemanship*, I, 144.

Barker, who was standing and racing the horse. So he knew the strain. When Maxwell told Blake that he had a Cold Deck colt for sale, Coke bought the horse sight unseen. Maxwell stayed on the ranch with Blake for nine years.

Blake bought Young Cold Deck in 1896 when he was an eight-year-old. His sire was, of course, Cold Deck and his dam a Bertrand mare. In 1898, Blake traded Young Cold Deck for the Joe Berry horse, also known as Berry's Cold Deck, that was a much better individual.

Joe Berry was a blacksmith who lived at Mt. Vernon, Missouri. The story of his horse goes like this. One day Jack Alsup, who at one time owned Old Cold Deck, brought Joe a mare to shoe. Joe shod her but got her lame in the process. Alsup was very unhappy, but philosophical. He asked Berry if he had enough sense to take the mare to Cold Deck to be bred if he should give her to him. Berry did. He led her the hundred miles to Old Cold Deck, and the resulting foal was the Joe Berry horse. Since Berry's Cold Deck was not a young horse when Blake traded for her, Blake got only about five years' service from him.

Blake bought his foundation White Lightning mares, four in number, from a dealer in Vinita. They had their start in Tennessee. The Alsup brothers were named Shelp, Lock, and Jack. They were well-known horsemen both in Tennessee, where they former-ly lived, and in Missouri, where they settled after the Civil War. Brother Jack went back into Tennessee and confiscated White Lightning without bothering to ask his owner. He rode the horse back to his home in Missouri. When a sheriff and deputy showed up to arrest Jack and get the horse, Lock shot the sheriff. The deputy escaped but got together some more men and returned. When the shooting ended, Shelp and Lock were dead. Jack, how-ever, managed to escape with White Lightning.

Blake got his Brimmer blood through N. B. Maxwell. Maxwell owned a Brimmer mare that Blake claimed was the fastest he ever saw, she stood 14–1, weighed 1,200 pounds, and wore a 00 shoe. She had a stride of nineteen feet. Blake offered Maxwell $1,000 for her. Blake bred Lucy Maxwell, as he called the mare, to the

128

Joe Berry horse in 1902, and in 1903 Tu-bal-cain was foaled. Tu-bal-cain was the best stallion Blake raised.

The story Blake tells about how he discovered he had raised a great horse is interesting. One day a rainstorm came up unexpectedly, and he heard his horses running for the barn. He got up and went outside, and by the time he could see the barn, they were all inside. He could hear one shaking himself, and it sounded like distant thunder. An old race horse man from Missouri had told him once that whenever a horse shook himself and it sounded like thunder, that was a truly great running horse. Blake ran to the barn to see what horse was making the noise. It was the horse colt Tu-bal-cain. Blake said old Tu-bal-cain had "the eye of an eagle and the step of a deer."

One of Tu-bal-cain's sons kicked the old horse in 1918, and he had to be destroyed. Blake then stood a son of Tu-bal-cain he called Smuggler. The last stallion Blake had was Ambrose. He was by Shiloah and out of Lonesome by Blake's Traveler. Some of the better-known horses raised by Blake were Tu-bal-cain, Idle Jack, Red Man, Tramp, Smuggler, Shiloah, Old Red Buck, Smut, Old Baldy, Red Devil, Tubal Blake, and Billy Red.

DAN CASEMENT (1868)

For over half a century Dan D. Casement was a dominant figure in the livestock industry. When the Quarter Horse Association was being organized, he and his son Jack were as responsible as anyone else in seeing to it that the necessary leg work was done. He was a bulldog enthusiast who said over and over again that the reason for a studbook is to preserve the physical characteristics of the Steel Dust.

Dan Casement's father was the General John Stephen Casement who was instrumental in building the Union Pacific across the continent. Dan claimed his father had the first steer herd to graze on the northern great plains. When Dan was ten years old, in 1878, his father acquired land in the valley of the Big Blue, four miles north of Manhattan, Kansas. Soon after he added two thousand more acres and stocked the ranch with cattle. A few years later the General appropriated a ranch in the Unaweep Canyon of western Colorado. The previous owners were the Uncompahgre Utes, who had broken camp and moved west into Utah Territory, which was not yet a state. The holding was located about thirty-five miles from Grand Junction about midway into the Unaweep Canyon. The headquarters was established on Fall Creek. Dan's first visit to the Unaweep took place when he was fifteen. He took the narrow-gauge from Denver to Whitewater, and then followed an almost nonexistent wagon road that wandered aimlessly some thirty miles up into the mountains, ending at the small cabin that was headquarters. The trail would have been more difficult to follow had it not been for the recent movement of the Utes. Their cast-off remains were visible here and there, such as broken tipi poles, discarded cooking ware, etc. The cabin was the origin of the Triangle Bar Ranch. Dan arrived in the early summer of 1883.

It did not take Dan Casement long to decide that he wanted to spend much of his life to come on the Unaweep; however, he returned home and continued his education, graduating from Princeton in 1891. At last he and his friend Tot Otis were making plans to go West together and run the cattle ranch. Mack Thomason became their foreman. Dan had first met him on a bear hunt in the Unaweep country.

Dan always had a special kinship with horses. You would almost have to say there was a mutual respect between them. Some of his feelings about horses come through in the following recollection he had of his early life on the Unaweep.

> The other horses in my immediate string were Navajo, Little Blue, and Grey Nelly the pack mare. The latter was of course, something of a nuisance in a remuda of geldings, but this was minimized by reason of her unfailing good manner, innate dignity and common sense. She was always helpful and patient. Often I packed a deer or a bear on her and sent her home alone over many miles of rough, timbered country. She attended strictly to her knitting. I was very fond of Nelly.[4]

Dan Casement remembered many horses with which he had had

[4] "From Punce to Deuce," *The American Hereford Journal*, July, 1954, 672.

contact. To him character was a vital characteristic in any horse. While he made allowances for a little more variation in horses than men, he demanded much from both. His admiration for one of his top mounts in the early days is evident from this further quotation from the same source. Speaking of Jack Paw, he said: "He was a finished cowhorse when I got him, and he did his best to make a competent cowhand out of me."[5]

After about five years on the Unaweep ranch, Dan's father asked him to go to Costa Rica with him to build a railway. Dan married his sweetheart, and they set sail for Costa Rica. They made their home in this Central American republic for six years. On his return to the States, Dan took up his residence in Colorado Springs, which was halfway between the family landholdings in Colorado and Kansas. This was in 1908.

Three years later Dan purchased Concho Colonel from William Anson and became, officially, a Quarter Horse breeder. When he returned from France at the end of World War I, he found he had too many Quarter Horses, all descendants of the Colonel. He advertised a sale in Grand Junction, and to his surprise there was a good market for his horses.

From this time on Dan Casement was well known, not only as a Hereford breeder and feeder but also as one of the best Quarter Horse breeders in the world. The story of his breeding operation is found elsewhere in this book. He died March 7, 1953, at Manhattan, Kansas, at the age of eighty-four.

OTT ADAMS (1869)

Ott Adams certainly rates as one of the best Quarter Horse breeders who ever lived. He was born in 1869 and died at the age of ninety-four in 1963. His name will always be associated with two great sires, one, Little Joe whom he bought, and the other, Joe Moore, whom he raised. Other well-known horses bred by Ott Adams are Zantanon, Lady of the Lake, Monita, Ben J, Adam, Stella Moore, Texas Rose, Kitty Wells, Smuggler, Boots, Jo-Etta, Jo-mo-ca, Grano de Oro, Pancho Villa, Clementia Garcia, Jim

[5] *Ibid.*

Wells, Pat Neff, Cotton Eyed Joe, Bumps, Joe Less, Lee Moore, Hobo, and others too numerous to mention.

Ott was born and raised in Llano County, Texas, but moved to and lived in Jim Wells County most of his life. He was the son of Bob and Helen Adams. His father had been born in England and his mother in South Carolina. Ott inherited his love of fast horses from his father, and as soon as he was old enough to go on his own, he moved to South Texas and settled on a small ranch near Alfred. Here he learned about the South Texas Quarter Horse from Dow and Will Shely, who owned Traveler and were to breed King, Little Joe, and a dozen other well-known South Texas Billy horses.

The first horse he bought from the Shelys was El Rey. A few years later he saw a Quarter Horse owned by George Clegg, called Little Joe, that made his mouth water. Little Joe, like El Rey, was by Traveler and bred by the Shelys. Ott made several trips to see Clegg in Alice before he was able to buy Little Joe.

Another purchase was Billy Sunday. Once when Ott Adams was being interviewed, he was asked specifically why he bought Billy Sunday. He said he had learned one thing for sure from Dow and Will Shely and that was how to judge a good horse. The only way to tell a good horse is by performance, he said. You can guess that to Ott performance meant speed. He said that in good years and bad you could always sell a fast horse. When horses were selling for fifty cents a head in this area, he was selling them for fifty dollars, and only because they were good ones that had speed. This, in brief, was his explanation for his success as a breeder.

Ott had no objection to conformation or beautiful heads or snappy colors; it was just that his main interest was in performance. He knew the futility of owning conformation without performance, something some modern breeders looking for purple show ribbons forget. When asked about conformation, he said that if you breed the fastest Billys (his word for Quarter Horses) together, the conformation you need will result. His horses certainly justified his belief. Of all the stallions he owned he liked Little Joe the best. Billy Sunday he liked, but not the same way he did Little Joe. Ott also bred some mares to Hickory Bill, another son of Peter McCue that George Clegg owned for a while. Ott himself had the best luck using Little Joe on the top line and crossing him on mares by, or closely related to, Rondo, John Crowder, Peter McCue, or Chicaro. Ott was once asked which horse he considered the greatest he had ever seen, and he had seen Bold Venture (the great Thoroughbred son of St. German), Chicaro, Rondo, Ace of Hearts, and Hickory Bill. He never paused to consider, but said Rondo was the greatest.[6]

Two of Ott's best-known sayings were that the only way to get speed is to breed speed to speed and a Quarter Horse can run his best for as long as he can hold his breath. Certainly he had this first axiom in mind when he bought Della Moore to breed to Little Joe. The result was Joe Moore, who was foaled on the Adams ranch in 1926. Ott later sold Little Joe, but when Joe died he got him back and buried him under a locust tree planted a hundred years before by Ott's mother. When Joe Moore died in 1961, Ott placed his remains beside those of his sire.

Ott Adams was a small man who looked as if he might have been a jockey, but he never had been. His philosophy of raising good horses was absurdly simple. Buy the fastest horse you can which belongs to your breed.

Ken Fratis once said something that was typical of all that was good about Traveler, Possum, and Little Joe colts. In speaking of Joe Moore, he said that he always impressed him because no matter when or where he stopped, he was always standing square with his feet under him.

Ott Adams very seldom bred an outside mare to Little Joe or Joe Moore. He accumulated a small but choice band of mares, most of which he had raised himself. The horses he selected to be the sires of his mares were Chicaro Bill, Paul El, Billy Sunday, Spokane, and Sam King. It was a Chicaro mare that foaled Stella Moore.

The closest Ott ever came to breeding to a Thoroughbred must have occurred when he bred a West Texas mare named Juanita.

6 Ott Adams wrote very little, but he was always ready to talk. One article credited to him, but with the help of Nelson Nye, is "Breeding Quarter Horses," *Texas Livestock Journal*, May, 1949, and another, with the assistance of A. C. Allen, was "Credit Given to Shelys," *Western Livestock*, August, 1945.

Juanita, whether Ott knew it or not, was by Priory, a Thorough-bred. The offspring was the famous Monita. Ott Adams considered breeding to a Thoroughbred as breeding down. He liked to say that every time you put another Thoroughbred in there, you take some-thing off your quick start. In Ott's day, with no gates and little train-ing and races run short distances, a start was everything. The ranch-ers, too, wanted a fast start so that they would not have to run all the beef off their stock before they could catch or turn them.

A Spokane mare produced Lee Moore, whom Ott considered Joe Moore's best colt. South Texas has had many great Quarter Horse breeders, but none greater than the big little man from Al-fred, Ott Adams.

WILLIAM ANSON (1872)

The first man in modern times to promote the Quarter Horse was William Anson. By birth he was an Englishman, by preference a Texan. His articles on Quarter Horse history were the first to dem-onstrate the Colonial origin of the Quarter Horse. He settled at Christoval, Texas, in 1893. There, on land lying a few miles along the Sonora road from San Angelo, he created a beautiful ranch. Giant bubbling springs, which form a major source for the South Fork of the Concho River, furnish a perpetual supply of cool, clear water for the ranch.

Anson had been a polo player of note in England, and naturally he wished to continue the sport at his new home. When he saw an animal he liked, he would ask about its breeding. Many of the horses he liked best had a strain of "Quarter blood," a new term to him. Being of a curious nature, he wanted to find out all he could about this new equine type. Let him tell it in his own words:

> When I first came to Texas, in most communities some man could be found with a stud of Quarter Horses and short distance racing was popular. As I had accumulated a certain amount of knowledge about breeds and breeding and the laws of heredity I realized that the Quarter Horse was not the result of a chance lot of ponies, just picked up and bred because of aptitude for speed at short distances. The type was so uniform and characteristics

134

so marked, that it became evident to me that here must be some old established breed. Quarter Horses interested the old timers I knew in those days. They had lots to tell me about Steel Dust and other well known racing stallions and mares, but they knew nothing beyond the fact that most came from Missouri, Illinois or Tennessee. Then I came across a quotation in Wallace's *Horse of America* which led to further investigation. Quite a few statements about Quarter Horses, some definite and others from which inferences are drawn, are found in many old horse books, making frequent reference in one way or another to the Quarter Horse and quarter mile racing in Virginia and Carolina.[7] . . .

The most conclusive proof that the pedigree of many families in *The American Stud Book* as stated by Bruce, trace back to the Quarter Horse, is Edgar's *Stud Book*, the first and only volume of which was published about 1832. Edgar's book includes the name and pedigree of many animals that he calls Quarter Horses. When Bruce compiled *The American Stud Book*, he used the same names and pedigree but failed to note that the animals were Quarter Horses.[8]

The first Quarter Horse Anson bought was from one of the old-time breeders in the San Angelo area, Alex Gardner. From Alex he purchased Jim Ned, a Billy horse sired by Pancho. Gardner had come to San Angelo from Zavala County, Texas, in 1882, and soon became famous for his two stallions, Pancho and Joe Collins. It is said that Gardner kept $1,000 posted at all times for anyone who wanted to run Pancho any distance up to a quarter of a mile. He was never beaten. In the beginning Anson did not think of Jim Ned as the stallion he would want when he began breeding; he was more interested in him as a representative of a breed new to him. However, as his contact with Quarter Horses widened, both on the ranch and on the polo field, he began to change his mind.

[7] This quotation is taken from Anson's notebook, a copy of which is in *Denhardt Files*, Anson Folder 3.

[8] "About the Quarter Horse," *The Breeders' Gazette*, August, 1922. Anson published a small booklet containing the results of his research and breeding activities. On the title page is found the following: *Breeding a Rough Country Horse*, by W. Anson, Head of the River Ranch, Christoval, Texas, reprinted from *The Breeders' Gazette*, Chicago, 1910. For information of a more modern nature concerning his ranch and descendants, see Elmer Kelton's article, "Early Quarter Home to be Restocked," *The Quarter Horse Journal*, February, 1963.

When the Boer War broke out, the British government commissioned Anson to buy horses for the English cavalry. This turned out to be a break for Anson, because while he was buying horses for England, he was able to select some good Quarter mares he could use in his breeding program. All in all he purchased some 22,000 horses for England, and said he looked at no less than 100,000 individuals to buy that many. He purchased for himself around fifty head, and after getting them all together, he made a further cut until he had thirty left. Now he had what he considered a nucleus for a stud of Quarter Horses.

Here is what he had to say about his breeding experiences:

> In 1902, I bought an imported English polo pony stallion, from Eben, Jordan, and Hamlen of Boston. He was not in the stud book, but was very well bred being ⅞ pure blood. He was a complete failure. Then I bought another English polo pony stallion, which was accounted the best two-year-old of his year, Senior Wrangler, also seven parts Thoroughbred. He was as good a type Thoroughbred for any purpose as I could ask for, gentle as a dog himself, but when we came to break his colts we found they were not cow ponies or polo ponies. As far as he is concerned, I wasted several years in my breeding program.[9]

It was not long before Anson was convinced that using Thoroughbred blood was not the way to breed the kind of horse he wanted. He began to look for additional suitable Quarter Horse blood to breed to his mares. In 1907, he bought a stallion by Arch Oldham. Anson's attention was attracted to Arch Oldham when he saw a beautiful mare by this stallion which took second prize in the open class at the Meadowbrook Polo Pony Show in September of 1907. As soon as he returned to Texas, he looked up Arch Oldham and bought a colt named Crawford Sykes sired by Arch Oldham. The colt got its name because its dam was bred by the famous Quarter Horse breeder, Crawford Sykes. The next year Anson bought Harmon Baker. Two years later he purchased his third stallion, the seventeen-year-old Sam Jones.

[9] This quotation is taken from Anson's notebook, *Denhardt Files*, Anson Folder 3.

Harmon Baker [said Anson], who is thought more of than any horse since the days of Steel Dust, has just the right mixture, and perpetuates his own wonderful conformation and disposition more truly than any stallion I ever knew. I cannot remember the exact date, but he ran a race in Oklahoma City, somewhere in 1911, 1912 or 1913. There was a short race on the program every day. They offered one particular purse for a three furlong race which attracted race ponies from Kansas, Illinois, Oklahoma and Texas (12 entries). They knew Harmon would win if left to himself, and a horse was put in for the purpose, which was accomplished, of knocking him off his feet at the start, for which the jockey was set down for the rest of the meeting. Almost, you might say, left at the post, he came through and won in 34¼ seconds. I never race him myself. I let a reliable man take him out after the breeding season is over, just to let him make a reputation and his name has become a household word among Texas Horsemen.

Jim Ned, my original purchase, is a beautiful brown horse, about 14.3, and weighing about 1100 pounds. For twelve years he has served me faithfully, out in the pasture during the summer months with his mares, and the remainder of the time in the saddle horse pasture, doing as much or more work than any cowpony on the ranch; he is a true representative of a great race. Even tempered and intelligent, easily kept, never ailing or sick for a day, sure footed and never known to be guilty of a mean act or trick, this is the horse which has laid the foundation of my stud. The other stallions in service, were, it is needless to say, selected with the same object in view; they are being bred principally to mares sired by Old Jim, as he is affectionately known on the Ranch.[10]

Harmon Baker is so well known that little need be said about him. Five of his sons gained well-deserved reputations; namely Dodger, New Mexico Little Joe, Harmon Baker, Jr., Harmon Baker Star, and Jazz. Modern-day blood, for the most part, goes back to Jim Ned by way of Concho Colonel, Dan Casement's great stallion, and through his descendants Red Dog, Billy Byrne, and Frosty.

Blood of Anson's stallions can be found in almost every one of

10 *Ibid.*

the bloodlines of the early breeders. Certainly Anson can be considered the dean of the Quarter Horse industry. He died in 1926, and his horses were sold.

GEORGE CLEGG (1873)

For many years the best-known breeder of Quarter Horses in Texas was George Clegg, of Alice.[11] One reason he was so widely known was that many of his horses had become foundation stock in the neighboring states of Arizona, New Mexico, and Oklahoma.

George Clegg was born in the Mission Valley of Texas about halfway between Cuero and Victoria, on April 2, 1872. He was the son of Austin and Dora Power Clegg. His father came from Van Buren, Arkansas, and his mother's parents came from Ireland. In 1904, George moved to Alice and began to concentrate on horses instead of steers, which he had been raising on leased land in Duval County. Perhaps Clegg's outstanding work was the skillful blending of two strains of Quarter Horses, those known as Rondos or Billys with the Watkins' horses of St. Petersburg, Illinois.

George Clegg was always interested in riding and roping and spent a lot of his time roping steers. One day Clay McGonigal came into that area on his good Quarter Horse Scooter and pretty well cleaned up the local boys. After this experience, Clegg saw that he had to have faster horses, and he decided to obtain and raise the best Quarter Horses available in the United States. The Rondo horses were the best in his area. He had heard quite a bit about the horses belonging to Frank Wiley, of Cuero, Texas. Going to Cuero, he looked up Wiley and purchased Little Rondo, whom he used for a number of years, finally selling him to Sam Lane, of Hebbronville. After selling Little Rondo, he had to find another stallion to go on his Rondo mares, so he purchased Little Joe from Dow Shely. When Little Joe outran Carrie Nation in his first race in San Antonio in 1908, Clegg was most satisfied with his purchase. Later

11 Two different, but good accounts about George Clegg may be found in Bob Hunter's article, "George Clegg, Veteran Breeder of Top Quarter Horses," *Western Livestock Journal*, May, 1941, and in Garford Wilkinson's, "George Clegg, Pioneer Breeder of Top Quarter Horses," *The Quarter Horse Journal*, January, 1959.

Clegg sold Little Joe to Ott Adams, of Alfred, Texas, and began looking around for another stallion to replace him. Clegg had been hearing a great deal about the horses owned by the Watkins family of Illinois. The Trammells and Newmans, of Sweetwater, had bought Barney Owens and Dan Tucker from them, and William Anson, of Christoval, had bought Harmon Baker. Their Peter McCue had been in San Antonio and had impressed many people.

Clegg's desire to get a good animal from the Watkinses was further encouraged by contact with one Pap Rebo, a jockey who had worked in Illinois for Watkins and who was now riding horses for George Clegg. The opportunity came after the death of the senior Watkins when at an estate sale Clegg bought a sire which was to produce his greatest horses. He bought Hickory Bill, a son of Peter McCue. He also purchased two great mares, Lucretia M, who was the dam of Hickory Bill, and Hattie W, who was to become the dam of Cotton Eyed Joe. Clegg then began to breed Hickory Bill to his Rondo mares and to fillies by Little Joe out of Rondo mares, and this cross produced some of the greatest horses to come out of south Texas. Some of these horses were Old Sorrel, famous foundation animal of the King Ranch, Paul El, who sired Spokane, and Sam Watkins, who sired Coon Dog. Clegg finally sold Hickory Bill to John Kennedy. The stallion died in 1923.

George Clegg was an outstanding Quarter Horse breeder for almost fifty years, and a surprising percentage of the performing Quarter Horses in the United States trace back to horses which he bred. George Austin Clegg died in Alice at the age of eighty-six.

COKE T. ROBERDS (1875)

Some years before the Civil War, a colony of settlers from Tennessee, Kentucky, and the Carolinas moved bag and baggage into Texas and settled along the Brazos River. Among the group was G. O. Roberds and his new wife. As the years rolled on, six children were born, one of the last, born in the 1870's, named Coke T. Roberds. The family moved to Trinidad, Colorado, while Coke was still a boy.

About twenty miles east of Trinidad the elder Roberds bought a ranch, where he raised large herds of horses as well as cattle. Coke grew up with a rope in his hand and his feet in stirrups. He attended high school in Trinidad and was sent east to college. Like Dan Casement, one of his friends and colleagues, he soon decided that town work was not to his liking, and began looking for a job on a ranch. He found one in West Texas, and also a wife, for he married there in 1898.

Within a few years farming began to replace ranching in the area, and Coke decided to move into a better country. He selected Western Oklahoma. When he moved, he took what horses and cattle he had accumulated with him. He began breeding Quarter Horses in 1898. A man had come by his place one day with nine Steel Dust mares that he liked and bought. They furnished the foundation on which he commenced his breeding program.

His next problem was to find a suitable stallion to use on these mares. He remembered having seen some horses in Denver which he felt would be satisfactory. They were owned by Senator Borilla, of Trinidad, Colorado, who was one of the best breeders west of the Mississippi River. The stallion that Coke bought—Primero by name—was a half brother to the famous Colorado Senator, a stallion sired by Leadville.

Don Flint, writing about Coke's horses, quotes him as saying, "When I started with the few head of Steel Dust mares and Primero, it never entered my mind about selling any of the offspring—just thought I would raise a few to ride after cattle, but have sold quite a few since."[12] After a few years of ranching in Western Oklahoma, Coke decided to move farther north to find better grass and more water. He decided on Hayden, Colorado. It was not easy to move in those days. He had to ship by the Rio Grande Railroad to Wolcott, then drive his livestock and freight his baggage north over the mountains.

In the move, in 1908, as fate would have it, the train was wrecked and Primero was killed. With the loss of Primero, Roberds was again faced with the problem of selecting the proper stallion

12 "Coke T. Roberds," *The Western Horseman*, November, 1946.

to go with his brood mares. At this point he had a stroke of luck. He came into the possession of Old Fred.

The background of Old Fred, as outlined in another section of this book, is rather hazy. Probably the truth of the matter is that nobody knows the truth, as Roberds maintained.[13] However, other individuals who possessed offspring of this great horse, Old Fred, made prolonged investigations and were led to believe that he came from Missouri and was sired by Black Ball, an outstanding Quarter Horse of that state.[14]

The next great sire to be used by Coke Roberds was the immortal Peter McCue. Si Dawson and his brother-in-law Coke Roberds were talking about stallions one day, and Dawson was very enthusiastic about Peter McCue and his offspring. He thought they could very well use a Peter McCue stallion in that area of Colorado and was all for buying a son. Coke's reply was that the wisest thing to do would be to buy the old horse and have the fountainhead, so Si Dawson went to Texas and purchased Peter McCue and brought him to Coke's ranch. Coke now had the stallion which was to produce some of the greatest Quarter Horses ever seen in the Rocky Mountain region, especially when bred to mares by Old Fred or when Old Fred was bred to Peter McCue mares. Shiek and Buck Thomas were among the notable horses produced. Buck Thomas was soon sold to the Waggoner ranch in Texas, where he sired such progeny as Bill Thomas and Red Buck. Another great individual, a daughter of Old Fred out of a Peter McCue mare was Squaw, who had a remarkable career on the short tracks, winning forty-nine out of fifty starts; she then continued as an unforgettable brood mare.

Coke Roberds was a horseman to the core and in his younger days he was an outstanding roper. He always insisted on good cattle and good horses, and his ability to breed both was phenomenal. Evelyn P. Semoten, writing in *The Quarter Horse Journal*, said all that really needs saying about Coke:

13 Roberds told the author in 1939 that he never could find out how Old Fred was bred, and that nobody he knew could tell him. *Denhardt Files*, Roberds Folder.

14 Mrs. Evelyn P. Semotan is a case in point. See her article "Old Fred, A Famed Stud," *The Quarter Horse Journal*, December, 1955.

We in the Quarter Horse business owe a great deal to Mr. Roberds for his long time of raising good horses and passing on to us the great nick that he made. It was a lucky day that he bought Old Fred in the middle of the road and luckier when he decided to buy the old Peter McCue instead of one of his sons.[15]

Coke Roberds died in 1960 at the age of ninety while visiting his niece on the Kelvin Ranch near Santa Fe, New Mexico.

[15] *Ibid.*

10. STARTING THE AQHA

THERE WOULD NOT HAVE BEEN an organization if a few dedicated persons had not been willing to put their shoulders to the wheel. It was my good fortune to find breeders who had the means at hand and the desire to do what was necessary. This desire was fed by a deep love for the old-time Quarter Horse.

My own interest in cow horses in general and the Quarter Horse in particular began in the early 1930's, but it was not until I started to teach at the Agricultural and Mechanical College of Texas that I was able to do much about it. Since my parents lived in California, the trip back and forth from Texas, through Arizona, New Mexico, Colorado, Oklahoma, Kansas and any other state that might have the right kind of horses, provided ample opportunity to visit breeders throughout the West.

One of the first and certainly best contacts was with Jack Casement in Colorado. He was the most articulate of the stockmen desiring a Steel Dust studbook. He and his father, Dan D. Casement, were outstanding breeders of Quarter Horses at the time.

On trips through Arizona I became acquainted with Ernest Browning, W. D. Wear, A. A. Nichols, and other early breeders. In New Mexico, with Elmer Hepler, J. W. Shoemaker, Albert Mitchell, Curtis Sears, Ed Springer, Milo Burlingame, and John Zurich. Oklahoma was an especially fertile field with men like Bert Benear, Jim Minnick, John Dawson, Coke Blake, J. V. Frye, A. E. Harper, A. I. Hunt, Bob Weimer, and Ronald Mason.

In Colorado and Wyoming interesting days were spent with Coke Roberds, King Merritt, Hugh Bennett, and Marshall Peavy. It is difficult to mention Texas, because here I could travel and

143

visit every holiday and week end. Some men, like J. Frank Dobie, Raymond Dickson, and Tom Hogg, never became active in the association but always went out of their way to help find Quarter Horses and their breeders.

The two men in Texas who most impressed me, not only because of the quality of their horses but also because of their sincerity and devotion to the Quarter Horse, were Jack Hutchins and Lee Underwood. The fact that both had oil wells and were without financial worries of the normal variety was also a considerable asset. In any case, Jack and Lee became my closest companions and advisers in the organization of the AQHA. We were collectively responsible for the errors and advances made during the first few years at least until 1941 or 1942.

The people who stood behind us all the way were Ott Adams, Frank Austin, C. K. Boyt, R. A. Brown, John Burns, Ray Canada, O. W. Cardwell, George Clegg, J. D. Cowsert, Jess Hankins, Jim Hall, Bob Kleberg, Helen and Max Michaelis, Roy Parks, Bill Warren, Cuter Wardlaw, and D. W. Williams.

This list, so far, includes most of those actively involved in the formation of the AQHA. A few others, handicapped by distance, did all and more asked of them—men like King Merrit of Wyoming, Hugh Bennett of Colorado, Orville Burtis of Kansas, and Melville Haskell of Arizona. It took many, and many were willing.

Quarter Horse breeders, such as those mentioned, made it possible for me to go ahead with the organization of a registry. The first meeting, called in 1939, was helpful but not fruitful. The second meeting, called for March, 1940, got the job done. The men who laid the foundation of the AQHA are well worth knowing better.

JACK HUTCHINS

Jack Hutchins was the son of a country doctor who lived at Weimer, Texas. His early education was limited, but he continued his own education until he knew more than the dozen or so accountants, tax experts, agricultural specialists, and petroleum engineers he later employed in his widely diversified business interests.

While still a boy, Jack became interested in telegraphy, much as

144

boys today become interested in radio or television. Soon he was a skillful operator and went to work for the Southern Pacific Railroad. Before long he found himself at a small "whistle stop" in South Texas. There he saw many cattlemen, including the great Shanghai Pierce, already a western legend. Shanghai, in the 1880's, had established his headquarters at a place he called Pierce. He and his brother Jonathan owned most of the country between Wharton and Matagorda Bay.

When the Southern Pacific built a station near his place, Shanghai furnished the material. He happened along when a painter was blocking out the word "Pierce" for the station sign. He looked at the sign for a moment and shouted, "I bought the lumber for this station, now put the other letters up there." The workman obeyed and the sign became "Pierce's." It was in this station that Jack went to work. Shanghai died in 1900, and his nephew, A. P. Borden, managed the estate.

One day Borden came into the station and said, "Son, how much do they pay you here?" When Jack told him, A. P. replied, "Why, lad, I'll pay you that much to carry my briefcase." Jack carried it so well that by 1937 he was manager of the Pierce estate at a fabulous salary; even before becoming manager, he had purchased a substantial interest in the ranch. There were about three hundred producing oil wells on the estate at that time.

Jack owned five outstanding Quarter Horse stallions. They were Lobo, Billy, Joe Louis, Bill Thomas, and Humdinger. He also had short-running horses whose blood was incidental to their ability to produce speed. They were Babe Ruth and Danger Boy, both sons of Flying Bob. He had also some wonderful mares; these too were divided into Quarter mares and race mares. Outstanding among the Quarter mares were Lightfoot, Chili Bean, Ginger Reed, Cimarron, and Mexico Lady; and Skippy, Mae West, Black Beauty, Annie, and Rosedale, among his racing string.

Lobo had been given to Jack by his friend Raymond Dickson. Lobo was by Spokane by Paul El by Hickory Bill. Bill Thomas was by Buck Thomas by Peter McCue. Humdinger was by Norfleet by Sparkplug. Billy was by Grano de Oro by Little Joe. Grano de Oro

145

and Billy were owned by Jack's neighbor and friend, Mentor Northington. Mentor gave Billy to Jack. The day before Jack died he gave Billy back to Mentor, a thoughtful gesture that touched Mentor deeply. Billy, along with Ott Adams' Joe Moore, was one of the truly representative individuals of the Billy horse breed. Both were examples of the caliber of horse we had in mind when the AQHA was formed.

It was typical of Jack that he would not let us register any of his horses on the first go-round. He wanted everyone else to have the first chance. That is why the last forty-four registrations in the first studbook are his.

Jack's breeding interests were twofold. His registered Quarter Horses were the using horses for his ranch operations. His hobby was running short races, and his desire was to have faster horses than his neighbors. He bought the fastest short-horses he could find. Johnny Ferguson was his partner, and between them they got together some of the best Flying Bob colts and fillies in the country. They secured the services of several Louisiana trainers and jockeys, such as Boyd and Paul Simar, and Pat Castile.

The author counseled with Jack before every move while the AQHA was being organized. Jack had a God-given gift that was in many ways the key to his character, to which the AQHA owes a tremendous debt. It was his ability to solve tough problems. The trees never kept him from seeing the forest. He would ask four or five pertinent questions, and when these questions were properly answered, the solution to the main problem became obvious. It was partly his ability to see alternatives—and when one knows the alternatives, choice is generally easy. Of course, one has to be able to eliminate all the unimportant and confusing related items, and Jack was a master at doing so.

Many who read this will recall one of our earlier conventions when debate waxed hot and heavy over certain issues. People were resigning, shouting, glaring, or questioning one another's honesty or motives. The president, Lee Underwood, had a light heart attack and was helped from the room. Jack took over. Quiet descended. In a droll sort of way he chastised the members of the assembly for

146

their unseemly actions, cleared the scene by reminding them that the argument was not over who owned how much stock, or who could vote how much, but over what was "good or bad for the Quarter Horse." Everyone relaxed, felt a little sheepish about arguing over stock, voting methods, and other things when the question was a simple registration rule change. Needless to say, Jack saved the day. The argument had been about everything except the question at hand.

Jack's reactions to the A, B, C classifications as set up at an executive committee meeting at Lee Underwood's Windthorst Ranch was typical. "Well, boys," he said, "you are all for it so I'll not vote against it, but it will never work." The next day on the way home he told me that we had seen the beginning of the end of the bulldogs. As usual he was right. To Jack a Quarter Horse was a Quarter Horse, a Thoroughbred a Thoroughbred, and a half-breed neither. Knowing his feelings, I once asked why he ran horses with Thoroughbred blood. "To win," was Jack's answer, "but you will not find my racing string mixed with my Quarter Horses, nor will you find my cowboys riding race horses." With the single exception of Joe Louis, a little Quarter stallion that could run, he bred his race mares strictly to his racing stallions.

Examples of his assistance to me and to the organization are almost too numerous to mention. The first time a meeting of the Quarter Horse breeders was called in 1939 at Fort Worth there were not enough present to warrant organizing. That spring Jack and I went over the list of breeders I had accumulated during the past few years. We decided to concentrate on a few individuals in each state, having them contact others, and to meet again in March, 1940, at the Fort Worth Fat Stock show.

Jack Hutchins went over the constitution which I had drawn up with Wayne Dinsmore's help and made several excellent suggestions, the key one being to set up the organization in such a way that the executive committee could run it. Since the directors were to be located all over the western United States, this suggestion allowed practical operation of the association. We sold stock at the meeting, but it all had to be purchased in advance. Jack per-

147

sonally bought most of it so that we could incorporate the AQHA, which we did in April, 1940. As new breeders wanted stock, Jack sold his. He never voted his big block of stock though he held over fifty per cent of the stock at one time.

Jack Hutchins was elected vice-president at the organizational meeting. Bill Warren, who was elected president, served two terms, then Jack was elected to this office in 1942 and again in 1943. By the close of Jack's first year as president, 1,287 horses had been registered, and there were many more applications pending. Because of the transportation difficulties during the war years, it was almost impossible for the inspectors to get around. They were volunteers who furnished their own gas, car, tires, and time. I don't know that the breeders ever have realized what a job Jack Hutchins and Helen Michaelis did during those two war years. They had inspectors in eight states, including four in Arizona, four in California, three in Colorado, twenty-five in Texas, and one in New Mexico, Oklahoma, Washington, and Wyoming. By the end of 1942 there were 279 breeders in sixteen states. Just two years before few breeders had even heard of a Quarter Horse, much less owned one! In fact, very few "life-long breeders" had any Quarter Horse blood in their strings of horses before 1940.

In March, 1943, the annual stockholders' meeting was held at the Blackstone Hotel in Fort Worth. It was voted to move the office to Eagle Pass, home of the secretary, so that she could keep abreast of the ever-expanding activities. The number of directors was increased to thirty. All officers were re-elected, leaving Jack Hutchins, president; Lee Underwood, first vice-president; Dan Casement, second vice-president; Jim Hall, treasurer, and Helen Michaelis, secretary.

Being president during these early years was not easy. The officers were striving desperately to register only good Quarter Horses, and many breeders were trying desperately to register every nag they owned because the market for registered Quarter Horses was booming. Many volunteer inspectors were more willing than able, more worried about hurting the feelings of the breeders than interested in the good of the Quarter Horse. Applications came in by the dozens on scrawny-hammed, roman-nosed, crooked-legged nags whose parentage was as nebulous as an alley cat's, but whose papers glowed with famous names of sires and grandsires who had not even been within missile-distance of the dam. Such applications when turned down caused great turmoil. During Jack's term his quiet manner and unequaled sense of justice kept things on an even keel.

Jack Hutchins died in the prime of life, killed by cancer, in July, 1945. No one will ever know what good he would have done had he been allowed to live.

LEE UNDERWOOD

It was generally conceded that R. L. Underwood had one of the most uniform band of Quarter mares at the time AQHA was organized. True, a few large ranches like the King Ranch had many top horses and perhaps even more acceptable bloodlines, but their breeding programs were primarily for their own use, and their major interest was not in raising Quarter Horses but in general ranching activities. A few specialists—for example, Ronald Mason, King Merritt, Jack Casement, and J. W. Shoemaker—were raising superior horses with top bloodlines to sell for racing or rodeo purposes. Only Lee Underwood kept from fifty to sixty brood mares whose progeny were readily available to the public.

Robert Lee Underwood was born in 1887 and grew up in a great horse country, Haskell County, Texas. Farmers gradually began to displace the ranchers, and Lee Underwood became restless. He drifted through South and West Texas working as a cowpuncher, sometimes roaming as far as Arizona and New Mexico. In North Texas, he became acquainted with Colonel C. T. Herring, of Amarillo, and went on his payroll in 1912. Until the Colonel's death, Underwood worked for him in many capacities. When the Burkburnett oil field was booming, Colonel Herring staked Underwood, and in January of 1919 Underwood moved to Wichita Falls, where the Underwood Drilling Company was organized. At first the drilling was done largely for other oil companies, but by 1926 the Underwood Drilling Company had its own wells. Lee was the

149

principal stockholder and president and general manager for almost thirty years. In 1951 he sold a controlling interest in the company to his son, Clay Underwood. Nothing but a new shallow oil pool or a big-game hunting trip ever took him away from his beloved Quarter Horses for more than a day or so once he became financially independent.

Lee Underwood's success as a breeder could be due to three factors: His favorite stallion Chief, the band of sorrel mares he obtained of Mitchell and Zurick breeding, and his Joe Bailey mares. He would breed Chief to one of these mares, then breed Chief's son Dexter to the female produce. He would breed Dexter to Chief fillies and Chief to Dexter fillies. Only on the bottom line of his pedigrees can you normally find any outside blood. Occasionally he would inbreed as well as line breed.

Buddy Dexter, as an example, was sired by Dexter out of his half sister Little March. Wichita Dexter was by Dexter out of Sue Dexter who was by Dexter. Breeding as close as Lee Underwood did shows the strength of his stallions. Using outside blood only on the distaff side is dangerous except where an extremely sound and prepotent sire is used; otherwise weakness is magnified. The fact that the bulk of his breeding stock did not degenerate speaks worlds for Chief as an individual.

Chief was range-bred on one of Colonel Herring's ranches. The Colonel came to Archer County, Texas, in 1880, from Hill County, bringing horses of Copper Bottom strain with him. He ranched for a while in the Indian Territory. The Oklahoma land rush was too much for him, so he began buying land in North Texas. His headquarters were, for the most part, around Amarillo.

Working with Colonel Herring on his ranch gave Underwood an opportunity to select the best of hundreds of horses. By the time he was ready to raise his own horses, he had picked out the sire he wanted, Golden Chief. Golden Chief was a copper-colored sorrel with a red line down his back. He was not large, as stallions go, but clean limbed and beautifully proportioned.

Underwood was fortunate to able in 1936 to buy a group of Mitchell mares. The person who owned them at the time was

150

driving them across North Texas, and Underwood bought them on the spot. Under the circumstances, it was impossible to verify pedigrees. When AQHA was formed, he did everything possible to verify their breeding, and after many conferences and much letter writing, the pedigrees were as straight as they could be made. Albert Mitchell and John Zurick, the original breeders, and Underwood were satisfied that the breeding was substantially correct.

Some people think more of paper than they do of horses, but you can't ride a registration certificate, rope on it, cut on it, or race it. Before the formation of AQHA, pedigrees were of academic interest only and were of nebulous value except as a guide to probable origin and future breeding. That remains true. What counts is the produce—the Dexters, Billy Silvertones, Red Bobbie Reeds, Buddy Dexters, etc.

Lee Underwood also obtained several Weatherford Joe Bailey mares, the greatest of which was Rita Fiddler. First bred to Redwood, she produced Hellzapoppin, who was sold to Bill and John Warren in 1940. She then foaled Dimple Dexter, Rita Dexter, Bubble Dexter, Red Bubbles, Cherry Dexter, Romeo Dexter, Fiddle Dexter, and others. All told she foaled thirteen head, seven horse colts and six fillies. One of the better-known Dexter colts was Buddy Dexter, by Dexter out of Little March, who was by Dexter also. Buddy Dexter was a tremendous show horse. He won blue and purple ribbons almost every time shown and beat horses of the caliber of Poco Bueno in doing so. Buddy did equally well with other mares, producing some of his best get upon Chief mares.

Underwood's part in the organization of AQHA was of no little significance. In number of hours and dollars expended in the early efforts, he need not take a back seat to anyone. He was one of the three essential and responsible organizers. He never missed a meeting, never failed to complete any job he was asked to do, and never begrudged any time or money spent. The association owes him a tremendous vote of gratitude for his early efforts.

Some of the action and accomplishments of the association while Underwood was president are interesting. He was elected president on March 16, 1944, at the annual stockholders' meeting held in

151

the French Room of the Blackstone Hotel at Fort Worth. Officers elected with him were Dan Casement, first vice-president; Jim Hall, treasurer; and Helen Michaelis, secretary. On March 15, 1945, at the annual meeting at the Blackstone Hotel, he was re-elected president; R. A. Brown, first vice-president; Robert Denhardt, second vice-president; and Helen Michaelis secretary and treasurer. Wayne Dinsmore was the honored guest. By June the number three studbook was about ready for publication.

All was not peace and harmony, however. On the one hand the National Quarter Horse Association was causing a disturbance, while on the other a group of California horsemen were demanding radical changes. On February 6, 1946, a directors' meeting was held in Eagle Pass which will long be remembered. A list of some of the accomplishments indicate the heat generated. (1) The by-laws were amended requiring 50 per cent known Quarter Horse blood. (2) A charter for state organizations was drawn up. (3) Roy Parks was appointed to see about getting an office in Fort Worth. (4) An amendment prohibiting the registration of any horse with a spotted, pinto, appaloosa, or albino sire or dam was passed. (5) The *Permanent Stud Book* was to be opened after March 15, 1946. (6) Charters were issued to the Pacific Coast Quarter Horse Association and to the Montana-Wyoming group. (7) A committee consisting of Howell Smith, Bob Kleberg, Roy Parks, R. A. Brown, and Lee Underwood was appointed to approach John Burns to see if he would become the new secretary. Any one of these seven items was capable of causing a mild earthquake.

The subsequent annual meeting on March 14, at the Blackstone, was out of this world. It is doubtful that anyone there will ever forget that meeting. With the exception of Helen, who agreed to remain in office only until a new secretary could be found, all the officers resigned so that peace and harmony might be achieved. The new slate elected consisted of Albert Mitchell, president; Hugh Bennett, first vice-president; and Bob Hooper, second vice-president. Lee Underwood suffered a heart attack during the meeting and his health thereafter prohibited active work with the association.

JIM MINNICK

The financial success of the AQHA during its early days was due primarily to the work of Jim Minnick because he found so many horses to register. Also, to a large extent, Jim should be given the credit for the present conformation of the Quarter Horse. In his role of inspector he determined which animals were to be registered. He frankly admitted that he, as a polo player, preferred the half-breed type. He also pointed out that there would probably not be enough A type, or bulldogs, to finance the early operations of the AQHA. He therefore suggested to our executive committee that he be allowed to register three general types, A, B, and C, from the Steel Dust type to the half-Thoroughbred. By careful use of the A type, he pointed out, we could keep on breeding Steel Dusts.

The plan had some attractive features—most of them financial. We agreed. The end was foreseen only by Jack Hutchins. Naturally, once they were in the book, all horses, A, B, and C, became equal. Since the A's were scarce, the B's and C's were interbred and soon far outnumbered the original Steel Dust type. Since most breeders did not have Steel Dust type, it became popular to say they preferred the type they had.

Jim must have known every horseman in the United States. He was a life-long friend of Will Rogers. Both went to New York in 1905 to help Jack Mulhall put on the first rodeo held in Madison Square Garden. Tom Mix, Curtis Johnson, Jack Joyce, and other well-known figures were also there.

A few years later, Will Rogers and Jim Minnick took some horses to New York to sell. They had no luck and were soon broke and hungry. They went everywhere looking for a job. Jim was willing to settle for anything that might get them enough money to get home. Will held out. At last the Union Square Theater offered them twenty-five dollars for a show. The result was Will Rogers' first stage contract. Jim rode the horse on stage while

153

Rogers improvised some roping routines and talked when necessary to cover up any mistakes.

Jim was born on April 2, 1881, on a ranch where the old Chisholm Trail crosses the Brazos River in Texas. In 1903, he moved to a ranch in Foard County, near Crowell, Texas. It was here that he introduced the dude ranch idea to Texas. With a few cowboys, a cook, and a few tents he entertained sixteen paying guests from the East.

One of the guests had the misfortune to break a bone and was held up on the ranch. A couple years later this guest, Miss Della Halthousen, an eastern society girl, became Mrs. James H. Minnick. Jim's isolated ranch in the breaks of the Wichita must have seemed a far cry from New York and its environs. Here she brought up their family of five girls and one boy.

Mrs. Minnick had to run the ranch by herself much of the time because Jim was in Santa Barbara or on Long Island showing and selling polo ponies. He shipped many carloads from his ranch to Red Bank, New Jersey, where he maintained training quarters. It was here that he introduced actor Fred Stone and Will Rogers to polo.

Jim raised many excellent polo ponies from his Quarter Horse stallion, Colonel, perhaps the best being Red Angel. The Colonel was sired by New Mexico Little Joe, a grandson of Harmon Baker. Two other bloodlines popularized by Jim were Yellow Wolf and Waggoner Rainy Day. He also owned Bill Thomas and Humdinger before he sold them to Jack Hutchins.

Jim continued active in the affairs of the AQHA until his death in 1947. If the type of horse registered and the type of horse given the ribbons in shows has any effect on a breed, then Jim had considerable influence in the early days of the AQHA. He was the inspector and judge for all of the early horses.

BILL WARREN

William Barre Warren was born in Harris County, Texas, on October 13, 1904, and died in New Braunfels on April 9, 1949. He was a member of a distinguished ranch family; his grandfather, John

Warren, Jr., inherited a ranch and reared six children, four girls and two boys, Bill and John. Bill's father died in 1927, and he and his brother operated the extensive ranch holdings.

If Bill had one abiding passion in his life, it was to ride a better horse than any of his neighbors, and in South Texas that took some doing. Match racing and match roping were his hobbies, and he insisted on raising his own horses to work on and to race.

The two sires that Bill owned and liked best were Pancho and Alazan. Pancho was a brown stallion; Alazan a sorrel with a stocking on his rear leg. Pancho was by Paul El, by Hickory Bill, by Peter McCue, and was out of Black Annie, who was by Little Joe, by Traveler. Black Annie was a full sister of Pancho Villa, a name that will mean much to any old South Texas breeder. Alazan was a grandson of Ace of Hearts, by Cuadro, by Old Billy, and out of a daughter of Traveler. Bill's mares were in some ways better than his sires. For the most part, he had acquired them from George Clegg, John Almond, or John Dial.

When it came time to talk about a president for the organization being planned for owners of Quarter Horses, Bill seemed a logical choice. As a director of the Texas and Southwestern Cattle Raisers Association, he had prestige. As the friend of hundreds of rodeo, race, and ranch men, he would gain confidence for the new breed; and lastly, he lived at Hockley, near College Station, my home while I was secretary. Ease of communication and distances to be traveled were important points during the organizational period when planning sessions were desirable and when there was no one else to carry on the actual work and no money to hire a full-time employee. Once Bill was convinced that he should be our first president, the rest was routine. He was introduced to all of those invited into the association whom he did not know. All agreed that he would make an ideal president, and he did.

The AQHA was officially organized on March 15, 1940. Bill Warren was elected president; Jack Hutchins, first vice-president; Lee Underwood, second vice-president; Denhardt, secretary; and Jim Hall, treasurer.

On April 17, our charter as a nonprofit Texas corporation was

155

approved in Austin. Bill, Jack, and I spent no little time in Austin seeing that everything went smoothly.

By the time of our second annual meeting, in March of 1941, one thousand horses had been registered. Bill was re-elected, as were the other officers. In April, 1941, the National Stallions Board recognized the Quarter Horse as a breed. Bill watched over the new organization for two years and served it well and faithfully.

Helen Michaelis

Helen Michaelis held a position almost unparalleled in the livestock industry. She was one of the key figures in the organization and development of the modern Quarter Horse. I cannot think of another woman in livestock history who has played an equal role. Many women love cattle and horses. Many spend all of their time working livestock, but there has been only one Helen Michaelis.

Anyone who tries to explain a woman is doomed to failure, but some of the reasons for Helen's success can be analyzed. One reason so many women fail when attempting to talk horses with men is that they try to be like a man. Helen was always a lady, expected to be treated as such, and so always was. Had she tried to do, or be, something she was not, her vast knowledge of Quarter Horses would have been lost to the organizers, for she would not have been accepted in regular meetings.

Another reason for her acceptance, and indeed without which she would never have been inside the circle to begin with, was her profound knowledge of all phases of the Quarter Horse industry. As far as the AQHA was concerned, her whole life centered around Quarter Horses.

The third key to her unusual position was her background. Since she was brought up on a horse ranch, the language of horsemen was hers by birth. Horses were the consuming topic of conversation from the day she first began to talk.

Helen knew how to adjust. In the early days, when rules and regulations regarding registration had to be formulated from scratch, days and nights were spent at a ranch or hotel arguing and planning. Many ash trays were full and many glasses emptied

156

before the long meetings broke up. Such situations would have been impossible for a strait-laced, inflexible woman.

Another remarkable attribute was Helen's ability to give and take. She had an open mind, but if she felt she was right, it took a powerful argument to change her. However, Helen could disagree radically, even angrily, yet never resort to name-calling. Consequently we made her a full-fledged member of our group.

So much for an attempt to explain how a woman happened to be so instrumental in developing the AQHA. Let's just say it happened, and we are all the better for her help.

Helen's major contribution to the Quarter Horse began in March, 1942, when she was elected secretary of the AQHA. This is not to imply that she was not active earlier, only that the executive committee had to do the work. At that time the Michaelises were spending most of their time on their ranch in Coahuila, Mexico. When they leased the 02 Ranch south of Alpine, Helen's activities were increased.

Helen has had a most interesting life. It has been her good luck to do and have what she valued most. Life without a family, horses, or ranching would have been a prison to her, and she had all of these.

She was born Helen Mary Hall on a ranch in Kimble County, Texas. Her father, Fred S. Hall, had come to Texas from England to raise horses. Her mother was Florence Black, a daughter of Colonel William L. Black. Besides Helen, her parents had three boys, all younger than she. In 1917, the family moved to a better ranch in Concho County, near Eden.

When Helen was ready for college, she chose the University of Texas. It was not long until she had several irons in the fire. She spent the summer of 1928 teaching riding at Camp Ekalela near Estes Park in Colorado. When she came back to Texas, she had a bee in her "blue-bonnet." Rounding up the string of horses she had raised and trained on the ranch, she drove them overland from the ranch near Eden to Austin. At first she rented the Western Field Riding Club, but when she found herself with a going concern, she bought her own riding academy. By 1932 she had finished her

157

education and developed a good business. Then she fell in love, sold her stables (and all but a few horses), married Max G. Michaelis, Jr., and moved to Mexico with him.

Helen's interest in Quarter Horses did not, of course, start in 1940. My first contact with her was in the middle thirties. After reading one of my articles on the Billy horse of South Texas, she wrote me asking for more information on Ott Adams' Little Joe. It was obvious from her letter that she knew as much as anyone about South Texas horses. From that day on we were friends. She was one of the first persons invited to the meeting to organize a Quarter Horse studbook. She was elected a director and at the time of her death was one of the very few original directors remaining active.

No doubt the biggest problem Helen had to face grew out of the rule adopted by the association that in order to be registered a horse must qualify on bloodlines. Had Helen known less about bloodlines, the task might have been easier. Everyone who had a horse turned down on account of bloodlines after the inspector had passed it on performance and conformation felt he was being personally insulted. The very idea of having his horse rejected by some "woman who never even saw the horse"!

Ignoring indignant protests and appeals, Helen continued registering horses strictly according to the rules and regulations. The good of the breed prohibited any exceptions, and, believe me, each and every case was exceptional to the owner of a rejected horse. The war years and the requirement for pictures also contributed to the unrest. Although Helen loved the work, she had taken so much abuse that she was relieved when another secretary could be obtained. It should be mentioned here that she was not the only officer on the receiving end. The executive committee, composed of the officers, voted on each horse turned down, and they were equally responsible with Helen.

When someone's favorite horse was turned down—and we had to turn down more than we took—soon a restless and unhappy group emerged. We were receiving ultimatums on all sides. Therefore, at a private meeting, old officers decided to resign in March, 1946, hoping that a new slate and new start could afford greater chance of bringing the discordant groups into the fold. It worked. Helen was urged to stay on as secretary-treasurer until a replacement could be found, but a new start was made, and by giving a little here and taking a little there, the groups were once more united and old grudges healed. Melville Haskell and Albert Mitchell deserve most of the credit for bringing all the groups together into one Quarter Horse Association.

August 15, 1946, was Helen's last day as secretary-treasurer of the AQHA. She had given uncounted days and hours working for the association and, despite pressure and criticism, followed the rules and regulations to the letter. If we have a breed today, much of it is the result of Helen's work, for the formative years are the most critical, for men, beast, or registry. Helen died July 26, 1965, in Kyle, Texas.

BOB DENHARDT[1]

Over the past few years we have talked to a number of men who were in on the formation of the AQHA—breeders, ranchers, businessmen. Sometime during each conversation it became apparent that Bob Denhardt had done much more toward making the association possible than has ever been set down in black and white. We visited Bob at his home and after prodding and prying, were able to piece together a most unusual story.

Bob Denhardt's life has been a varied and unusual one. He was born and reared just a short distance from his present home in California and is a much younger *caballero* than a good many folks who have been seeing his name in print and reading his articles think. He was only twenty-eight when AQHA was incorporated.

He got his Bachelor of Arts sheepskin at the University of California, in 1936, and his Master's the next year at the same school. Naturally enough, his thesis was about horses—"Spanish Horses

---

[1] This section on Bob Denhardt was written by Randy Steffen for *The Quarter Horse Journal*, January, 1964, and permission for reproduction has been granted.

in North America, 1492–1542." This paper was the basis for his widely read book, *The Horse of the Americas*, published in 1947 by the University of Oklahoma Press.

While attending the University of California, he became well acquainted with Paul Albert, whose small Arabian stud was near Berkeley, and worked with him in getting out many of the first issues of *The Western Horseman*. There was a small group of horsemen in the area that shared Bob's interest in anything that had to do with the horse—Father Rivard, who wrote under the pen name of Don Alfredo; Dane Coolidge, the well-known western writer; Dick Halliday, the founder of the Palomino Horse Association; Francis Haines, who organized The Appaloosa Horse Association, and, as mentioned above, Paul Albert, the founder of *The Western Horseman*. This bunch of horse nuts sat up many a night talking about every phase of the western horse. Usually their headquarters was at Albert's Tarantula Ranch. This was during the Depression when there weren't many horse breeders, so Albert's outfit, with the stallion, Baraki, and a few Arab mares, was well known.

All these men had heard some about the legendary Steel Dust and his progeny that had established phenomenal reputations on the brush tracks of the cow country, yet no actual facts were known about the horse. When it became known that Denhardt was to teach at Texas Agricultural and Mechanical College, Paul Albert asked him to track down some concrete information on Steel Dust horses and do an article for *The Western Horseman*.

Up to that time very little had been written about the Western short-horses, but there was one article by a Colorado rancher which Bob had run across in his research for his thesis, "Colonel Concho, His Life and Times," in a 1927 edition of a cattle magazine. It had been written by Dan Casement, the owner of Colonel Concho, whose ranch was in the Unaweep Canyon country near Whitewater, Colorado.

A lover of good horseflesh, General Casement passed this trait to his son, and Dan to his son, Jack, who had some of the best horses in Colorado. Denhardt made a detour by way of the Casement ranch on his way to Texas A. & M. This was the beginning of a long friendship between Denhardt and Dan and Jack Casement.

During the next several years Bob visited every rancher in the Southwest who was reputed to have good Quarter Horses. And he learned an amazing fact: It appeared that the good horses being bred by men like the Dan Casements, Coke Roberds, Ott Adamses, and many more were all related. Some of the ancestors were called Steel Dust, others Billy horses, so Bob quickly developed a consuming interest in pedigrees.

It's interesting to note here that the owners of these good horses were not aware, for the most part, of this common relationship. At that time little effort was made to keep track of much more than a generation or two, at the most, of a good ranch horse's ancestry. Many of them were fast as greased lightning on the short brush tracks, and there were many matched races at the small fairs and rodeos throughout the Southwest. But it was the race horse man who predominated these meets, not the ranchers.

These men who made their living at the small tracks were not breeders. They made the rounds of the ranches known to have good horses, bought promising colts, trained them, and ran them. And these race horse men knew far more about the pedigrees of these ranch-raised sprinters than the breeders themselves. Denhardt was able to tie together many loose ends from information gleaned from the race track crowd.

Now a pattern began to take shape in his mind, and his thirst for more intimate knowledge of these good ranch horses and their origin became a consuming passion. On holidays, week ends, and all through summer vacations for the next few years Bob traveled from one end of the cow country to the other, always seeking information about the background of these good ranch horses, whose greatest fame came from their running on short tracks and whose greatest use was as working cow horses and in the rodeo arenas of the Southwest.

Both Jack and Dan Casement became interested in Bob's project right from the start, but both were working ranchers and were unable to spend the time at running down pedigrees that a young,

161

unmarried college professor could. And there were others who quickly saw the merits of Denhardt's theories on common ancestry, and who pitched in as much as busy schedules would allow.

At the time of his trip to Texas and his early visits to horse breeders in the Southwest, Bob had no thought of a breed association or registry in his mind. His interest stemmed from a long-time curiosity about the origin of the short horse—the Steel Dusts, and Billy horses, and others. But as time went on and he saw that almost all the great ones could be traced back to just a few individual stallions, the idea must have at least sprouted a tail.

Let's take a look at a few of the facts that some of these early trips during 1937, 1938 and 1939 uncovered:

The visit to the Casements in the summer of 1937, and subsequent stops there, revealed that Jack Casement's great horse, Red Dog, was sired by Balleymoony by Concho Colonel, a horse that Dan Casement had purchased from Uncle Billy Anson. Concho Colonel was by Jim Ned, Anson's famous stallion. Jack Casement is even now [1964] running great-grandsons and great-granddaughters of Red Dog, and doing real well. Red Dog's dam was a mare descended from Harmon Baker.

At Ernest Browning's ranch near Wilcox, Arizona, Denhardt found that Browning's good stallion, Red Cloud, had been sired by Red Dog.

Nearby, at the ranch of W. D. Wear, was Tony, a real well-put-together stallion sired by Guinea Pig by Possum by Traveler.

In New Mexico, Bob found that Warren Shoemaker was using and standing a powerful horse called Nick, who was by Sheik, a son of Peter McCue.

At Springer, New Mexico, he stayed a day or two at the Ed Springer outfit, and put another piece of his rapidly developing theory in place when he found that Ed's great horse, New Mexico Little Joe, was a son of Old Joe, who had been sired by Anson's Harmon Baker, himself an own son of Peter McCue.

In Colorado, Bob spent a few days at the ranch of Coke Roberds, the grand old man of the Quarter Horse world. Here, at

SHUE FLY
Defeating Rosita in a quarter-mile match race at Tucson, 1944.

DAN CASEMENT on The Deuce
The Quarter Horse owes much to this great American.

BALDY WITH TROY FORT UP
Many consider "Old Burnt Leg" the greatest gelding ever roped upon.

COURTESY SKEET RICHARDSON PHOTOS

OTT ADAMS
South Texas' great Quarter Horse breeder.

GEORGE CLEGG
Producer of some of the best horses
in South Texas' history.

WILLIAM ANSON
The first Texan to publicize
the Quarter Horse.

BILL WARREN and JIM MINNICK
On the left, Bill Warren, first president of the AQHA. On the right, Jim Minnick, director and the first inspector.

JACK HUTCHINS
Second president of the AQHA
and one of its prime organizers.

LEE UNDERWOOD
Third president and key figure in
the development of the AQHA.

THE FIRST SECRETARIES
Left to right, Raymond Hollingsworth, third secretary; Helen Michaelis,
second secretary; Robert M. Denhardt, first secretary.

Hayden, near Steamboat Springs, he found a breeding program featuring sons and daughters of Sheik, Old Fred, and Peter McCue.

Back in Texas, Denhardt found that Ott Adams at Alice had Joe Moore, a grandson of Traveler. And at Rocksprings, Jess Hankins owned a young horse that was to become a legend himself—King, a son of Zantanon by Traveler.

The pieces were fitting together. No matter where he went in the Southwest, Bob was finding that the outstanding horses could be traced back to two or three famous old-time short-horses. Up in Mayes County, Oklahoma, Coke Blake was extolling the quality of "The Famous Blake Horses," most of them sons and daughters of Tu-bal-cain, a stallion sired by Cold Deck, another of the famous old-time horses.

Si Dawson at Talala, Oklahoma, owned Little Earl, Jr., a grandson of Missouri Mike by Printer, and was running a bunch of Old Red Buck colts. Old Red Buck had been bought from Si by King Merritt of Federal, Wyoming, and at this time was standing at the Merritt ranch. Merritt's top steer-roping horse, Bullet, was by Jack McCue, a son of Peter McCue.

You can imagine how Bob Denhardt felt when all these facts fitted together to make it very evident that the short-legged, muscular horses that could do so much on the ranch and on the short tracks undoubtedly sprang from a mere handful of outstanding short-horse stallions. Here, then, was the evidence that germinated into the idea that a breed association could be formed for purpose of registering all the progeny of these existing good stallions and mares that were known to have descended from Steel Dust, Billy, Shiloh, and a very few others whose reputations as short-horses had been legend for years.

After that first visit to the Casements in 1937, Bob and Jack Casement visited again frequently. They agreed to write some articles for selected magazines and made plans for a future Steel Dust studbook, using the data Denhardt had uncovered showing the common relationship of so many good horses located in all parts of the cow country.

In the March–April, 1939, issue of *The Western Horseman* appeared an article by Jack Casement entitled, "Why A Steeldust Stud Book?" This was a sort of probe to see what other serious horsemen thought about the idea.

The first person Bob Denhardt knows who actually thought about doing a studbook to record the pedigrees of short-horses was Uncle Billy Anson, back around the turn of the century, twelve years before Bob was born. It was an article by Anson in *The Breeders' Gazette*, that provided him with the key to tracing bloodlines of the best Quarter Horse sires of the day back to the early Colonial days.

But Billy Anson couldn't spare the time necessary to track down other breeders and look up the pedigrees of their top horses in order to build up enough interest to warrant the time and expense a new breed registry would require. Thus, the idea was abandoned. And no wonder—Uncle Billy would have had to ride thousands of miles horseback. Bob commented, "I could travel from Oregon to South Texas while he was trotting across a few counties."

In the fall and early winter of 1939, articles by Denhardt appeared in horse and cattle magazines, creating a lot of new interest on the part of the horse breeders. "Peter McCue, Wonder Horse," in the October, 1939, issue of *The Cattleman*, is an example. It tied in almost all the outstanding bloodlines in the West to Peter McCue.

Another was, "New Light On Old Steeldust" in the November–December, 1939, issue of *The Western Horseman*. This was based on written records supplied by Coke Roberds, which let Bob remove, once and for all, the ancestry of many famous short-horse sires from the legendary status they had previously occupied. Steel Dust and Shiloh are two examples whose existence and parentage was authenticated.

The visits and contacts mentioned here that Denhardt made in the years preceding the formation of the American Quarter Horse Association are but a small percentage of the ranches and horsemen he sought out in his quest for firsthand information on the origin of the good horses of the West.

During an interview with Denhardt I asked just what kind of a horse was he looking for when he visited all those ranches, and was it the same type of Quarter Horse as is being registered today. He weighed his words carefully and then said, "That's a good question, and frankly, in many cases, Quarter Horses registered today would not have been considered good Quarter-type when the association was founded.

"I think the desire to have a race horse is as much at fault as any other single thing. If you want to produce a race horse . . . the easiest way is to cross a Thoroughbred, a horse that's been bred just for racing, and keep crossing him . . . on Quarter mares. You get a wonderful horse this way, for the Thoroughbred is the greatest race horse ever produced. He has more quality, size, and refinement than a Quarter Horse ever has had. But you lose if it's a Quarter Horse you want.

"We were looking for horses like Little Joe and Joe Moore, Balleymoony and Red Dog, Guinea Pig and Possum, Zantanon and King, Jack McCue and Bullet. They weren't Thoroughbreds, and they didn't look like Thoroughbreds—not even fat Thoroughbreds! They were small and compact, averaging about 14–3 and weighing from 1,050 to 1,200. They had good heads and big jaws, were rather short-necked and had medium withers. All were exceptionally well muscled, and it was probably this feature that first caught your eye.

"The muscles in their legs above the knees forked into a wide chest. Their hind legs were the kind you dream about, well muscled inside and out! Their knees were close to the ground and their cannons and pasterns were short.

"The tremendous heart-girth, coupled with short cannons and pasterns gave them one of their main characteristics—a bottom line that sloped down sharply to the front. We could always pick out a Quarter Horse in a corral full of Morgans, Arabs, Thoroughbreds, or any other breed! They were as unique in their conformation as they were in their ability to work cattle!"

The main thing Denhardt discovered during these years of running all over the country was the basis for organizing a breed

165

association and registry. The best Quarter Horses had a distinct type and common ancestors.

When he was satisfied that this was true, he began devoting every bit of his energy and persuasiveness and all the time he could spare from his schedule at Texas A. & M., to whipping up enthusiasm among the breeders.

In the spring of 1939, Bob had called a meeting of interested breeders for the express purpose of starting such an organization. This was in Fort Worth. But pressing business prevented all but a handful from showing up. Those who did attend decided to wait until the following year, giving them time to get others seriously interested.

Bob worked hard all that year—writing articles, visiting ranchers he knew would be good, reliable men to have in on the organization from the beginning and continuing his research into short-horse bloodlines.

Late that year and early in 1940, he wrote up a constitution and by-laws for a Quarter Horse Association. Wayne Dinsmore, president of the Horse and Mule Association, who had vast experience and knowledge of the operational problems of such an undertaking, looked over these first rules and helped revise them in places his experience deemed necessary.

Now it seemed as though the details for organization were in order. The time was ripe and Bob made an all-out effort to be sure the interested horsemen would be at the [second] meeting in Fort Worth in 1940. What happened that day is recorded history! The meeting was held at the Fort Worth Club in Fort Worth, Texas, and the horsemen showed up, rarin' to go!

Bill Warren, a rancher from Hockley, Texas, was elected AQHA's first president. A horseman all his life, he was interested in cow horses and in short racing. Jack Hutchins, one of the most enthusiastic supporters Bob Denhardt had, was elected first vice-president. Lee Underwood, Wichita Falls, was second vice-president. James Goodwin Hall, a lifelong horseman, was elected treasurer, and all those present made sure that a work-horse was nominated for the position of secretary—Bob Denhardt.

166

We've talked to people who were there, and in spite of his modesty and respect for the older heads, it was common knowledge that Bob Denhardt ramrodded that organization into existence! This is certainly not said to belittle the work done by Jack Casement, Jack Hutchins, Lee Underwood, and others. But Bob Denhardt was young, full of vigor, and he had the time to lay the groundwork. And so was born the American Quarter Horse Association.

GLOSSARY

ALBINO—A horse having little or no dark pigment in the skin or hair. He is generally white or light cream, with one or both eyes white or pink. Such an eye is variously known as a "glass," "watch," or "cotton" eye.

APPALOOSA—A horse having colored patches or spots on the rump. There is an organization to breed this animal, known as the Appaloosa Horse Club. It was organized in 1938.

AQHA—The American Quarter Horse Association, organized in 1940.

AQRA—The American Quarter Racing Association, organized in 1945.

ASK AND ANSWER—A method whereby two jockeys could start a race themselves. Each would bring his horse to the starting line and if ready would say, "Ready." If the other was also ready he would say, "go." The race was then on. Since both wanted the advantage, this was not the fastest way to start a race.

BAY—A horse color ranging from a light yellow to a dark red. A bay is easy to distinguish because he always has a black mane and tail. A sorrel never has a black mane or tail.

BIT—A metal bar that fits in a horse's mouth. It is fastened to the bridle and reins and insures that the horse will respond to the rider's wishes. SNAFFLE BIT. One that is hinged in the middle. SPADE BIT. One that has a high palate. CURB BIT. One that is curved into a U shape in the middle.

BLAZE—A wide white stripe extending down a horse's face.

BOTTOM—Ability to run a long distance.

BRITCHES—Used when speaking of the musculature of the rear quarters, especially of the gaskins, stifle, and thigh.

BROKE—Gentle to use.

BROWN—A horse color that often appears black. However the hairs on the muzzle and flanks are lighter on a brown horse. A black is black all over. The mane and tail are always black on both horses.

BRUSH TRACKS—Small private tracks in the rural areas of the West.

BULLDOGGING—A rodeo sport where a cowboy leaps from his horse, grasps the steer by the horns, and wrestles it to the ground.

CANNON—The long bone between the knee and the ankle or the hock and the ankle.

CAQRH—Celebrated American Quarter Running Horse. This designation was used by Edgar in his studbook to indicate the short-horses which he registered.

CAST—When a horse rolls in his stall and the wall prevents him from going all the way, and he is unable to turn back over or get up, it is said he is cast.

CHESTNUT—The Eastern term used for the sorrel color. Chestnut is not used in the West except to designate a deep dark sorrel, i.e., chestnut sorrel.

CHIN—To chin means to measure the height of a horse by placing your chin on his withers. When one knows the height of his chin, a very accurate measurement is possible.

CLEAN LEGS—This indicates that the horse's legs, especially from the knee or the hock down, show no wear and tear or unsoundness and are clean, smooth, and flat.

COLT—A young horse. HORSE COLT. A young gelding. FILLY COLT. A young female horse before being bred. STUD COLT. A young stallion.

COLD BLOODS—All race horses and most saddle horses are hotbloods. Draft horses are known as cold bloods. Hot-blood refers to Eastern or Arabian blood.

CONDITION—Health. Generally refers to a horse's readiness to run.

169

He is said to be in good condition. One in poor condition would not be ready.

CONFORMATION—The general appearance of a horse, including the balance between his head, body, and legs. The conformation of each breed varies.

CORONET—The line between the hoof and the pastern, where the horn and hair meet.

COW-MILKER—One who participates in the sport of cow-milking at a rodeo. This timed event consists of seeing who can first get milk from a group of wild cows.

CROUP—The highest portion of the curved area above the hips.

CURBS—A swelling apparent a few inches below the hock. It appears because of a strain or injury.

CUTTING HORSE—A horse trained to separate, or cut out, one animal from a herd. Since the cow does not like to leave, it takes ability on the part of the horse and the rider.

DAM—A female parent, just as the sire is the male parent.

DAYLIGHT, LENGTH OF—The gauge of victory in a race. If there is room for one horse's body between the first and second horse in the race, there is said to be one length of daylight.

DOGIE—A calf without a mother.

DRAWN DOWN—When a race horse is ready to run, all surplus fat has been removed and he seems thin and tucked up in the waist. This is called drawn down.

DUN HORSE—Dun is a horse color in which yellow hair predominates. The color varies from a pale yellow to a dark canvas color with some being almost blue. If it is golden with white mane and tail it is called a palomino. A zebra dun is one with black mane and tail and black zebra stripes on the legs. Many duns are lined back.

EWE-NECK—A horse's neck should arch slightly from withers to poll. When the neck is concave between withers and neck, the horse is said to be ewe-necked.

FEATHER—Hair around the fetlock is called feather, and indicates draft or cold blood.

170

FEET OF DAYLIGHT—(See Daylight, Length of.) The number of feet separating the first two horses in a race.

FETLOCK—A cushion-like projection on the underside of the joint above the pastern. The tuft of hair growing here is also called the fetlock.

FILLY—See Colt.

FLAX MANE AND TAIL—A white, or mostly light, mane and tail found on a horse with a darker colored body.

FOALED—Horse term meaning born.

FOREARM—The limb between the knee and the elbow or joint in the anterior leg of an animal.

FOUNDATION SIRE—One of the formative stallions of a breed whose prepotency is such that basic characteristics are faithfully transmitted for generations.

GASKIN—The muscle between the hock and the stifle.

GELDED—The state of being castrated.

GELDING—A castrated male horse.

GET—Progeny. A stallion has get; a mare has foals.

GLASS EYES—A white eye, one without dark pigment.

GO-ROUND—In most rodeo and cutting horse contests, each performer has more than one animal to ride, rope, or cut. When all contestants have worked, roped, or ridden one animal, it is called the first go-round. They then proceed to the second go-round.

GOOSE RUMP—Narrow croup or rear quarters of a horse which taper and droop below the tailhead. Referred to as goose-rumped.

HALF-BREED—A horse that is cross bred, having one parent belonging to one breed and the other to another. Often this term refers to a horse who has a Thoroughbred for one parent and a common horse for the other.

HAM DOWN—This term is used to designate a horse whose rear quarters are well muscled.

HANDS HIGH—Horses are measured in hands, each hand being four inches. The measurement is from the ground to the top of the withers.

HEAD, SOUTH TEXAS—A polite way to refer to the coarse head found on some South Texas horses. This is not a characteristic found only in South Texas.

HEART—Ability to continue running or working even when tired. In modern sports it is often called a second effort.

HOTBLOOD—Horses are generally divided into hotbloods and cold bloods. Hotbloods are horses tracing to the light breeds, especially the Arab. *See* Cold bloods.

HOOF—The horny growth that makes up the foot of the horse.

HOCK—The joint between the cannon bone and the fibula, or leg bone, of the horse.

INBRED—A horse whose parents are closely related. All horses are distantly related, but when father is bred to daughter, mother to son, or brother to sister, it is inbreeding.

IN THE MONEY—Placing first, second, or third in a race.

JAW, STEEL DUST—Steel Dust horses were characterized by large, prominent jawbones, that seemed to make their cheeks bulge. Many Quarter Horses still have this feature.

JINETE—A method of riding introduced into Europe by the Mohammedan conquest of Spain in 711. The position is somewhat similar to the jockey seat, well forward with short stirrups.

KNEE—The joint between the cannon and the forearm.

LAP-AND-TAP—A method of starting horses in a match race without gates. The judge starts (taps) them if they are lapped satisfactorily. If he doesn't start them they go back and come up to the starting line again. Ideally they are side by side, or lapped perfectly, when they reach the starting line.

LAPPED—When the bodies of two horses in a race overlap each other when viewed from the start or finish line. In other words, no daylight shows. A dead heat is perfect lapping.

LEADER, PULLED A—A leader is a tendon or ligament behind the cannon. When pulled or sprained, referred to as a bowed tendon, the horse is lame.

LEVELHEADED—Meaning a horse that is not excitable, but calm and quiet even under unusual circumstances.

172

LOIN—Muscles over the lumbar vertebra, just behind the rib cage and in front of the hips.

LONG-HORSE—A horse bred to run a mile or more, such as the Thoroughbred.

MOON BLINDNESS—A pale blue, or cloudy, watery eye is characteristic of periodic aphthalmia or moon blindness. The disease comes and goes but eventually results in blindness.

MUSTANG—Common name for the semiferal horses which lived on the great plains area in a wild state from the seventeenth century until the twentieth.

NAG—A derogatory name for a horse. It used to be used to designate a horse that was not well bred.

NOSE, ROMAN—When the flat surface of a horse's face between the eyes and the nose is convex it is said to be Roman-nosed.

NQHBA—National Quarter Horse Breeder's Association. A Quarter Horse Association which merged with the AQHA in 1950.

ON THE PULL—Means that a horse ran a race slower than necessary, being held back by the jockey.

OUTCROSS—When breeding to set desired characteristics, one uses the chosen blood almost exclusively. When a horse is inbred too much, weaknesses appear. To stop this, one can, occasionally, use an individual of a non-related family line. This is called an outcross.

OVERREACHING—When a horse hits one of his front feet with a rear, it is said to be overreaching.

PASTERN—The bone above the hoof and below the fetlock.

PACING—When a horse moves both legs on the same side in unison.

PALOMINO—A horse on which the hair appears a golden yellow and the mane and tail is white. The palomino has had a registry since 1937.

PINTO—A horse having two or more colors in rather large patches.

POLL—The top of the head.

REINING—Moving the horse, right, left, front or rear, by moving the reins.

REMOUNT STALLION—The army remount to supply fresh horses formerly stood stallions throughout the country, mostly Thoroughbreds. They were called remount stallions.

REMUDA—A group of saddle horses kept together on a ranch. In it are each cowboy's horses. They are customarily geldings.

ROAN—A horse color that has white hairs intermingled with one or more base colors. The amount of white hair changes with age. A small patch of white hairs does not make a roan. Much of the body must be roaned.

RUN FOR FUN BOYS—Ranchers or horsemen who race horses, occasionally, as a hobby. They also like to raise and train their own horses.

SCORED START—This is when the clock is started for a race after the horses have already run a certain distance. It gives the horses a running start. Quarter Horses are timed from a standing start, Thoroughbreds from a scored start.

SEAL-BROWN—A horse whose coat is shiny, dark, and dappled. *See also* Brown.

SESAMOID—A small bone at the rear juncture of the fetlock joint.

SHORT-HORSE—A horse bred to run a short distance, such as up to a quarter of a mile. A Quarter Horse is a short-horse.

SHOULDERS, ANGLE OF—The scapula, or shoulder bone of the horse is attached to the body only by a large cartilage. The angle of the shoulder should be about 45°. If it is too straight up and down the horse is rough to ride and subject to unsoundness. This is because the shoulder acts as a spring when it is on an angle.

SIRE—The stallion is known as the sire of the colt. The mare is the dam.

SNAFFLE—*See* bit.

SORREL—A horse color that is some shade of red. The mane and tail match the coat color, although they may have some white in them. A sorrel never has a black mane or tail.

SPRINTERS—A sprinter is a horse that runs best at distances under a mile.

STANDING START—*See* Scored Start.

STAYERS—A horse that runs best at a mile or more.

174

STRIDE—The distance from one hoof print to the next hoof print of the same foot. Normally measured when the horse is running.

STUDBOOK—A studbook is a registry for horses, listing both stallions and mares. You cannot have a breed without a studbook or registry since by definition all horses belonging to a breed must be registered.

SWAY-BACKED—A horse's back should be relatively straight from withers to croup. When the back is underly concave it is called sway-back.

THOROUGHBRED—A horse registered by The Jockey Club. The Thoroughbred is primarily a race horse and in his field is in a class by himself.

THROAT LATCH—The area on a horse's neck immediately behind the jawbones. It is where the head joins the neck.

TURF HORSE—A race horse.

USING HORSE—A riding animal used for some purpose other than pleasure or racing.

VAQUEROS—Mexican cowboys.

WALK-UP—In old match races, before gates where common, it was often necessary to walk the two horses up to a line drawn on the race path. If the heads reached the line together the starter would start the race.

WITHERS—A spinous growth on the backbone where the body joins the neck. The highest point on the horse's body.

WORKING FLESH—When a horse is not fat, but trim and in good condition.

BIBLIOGRAPHY

S INCE MOST OF THE READERS of this book will be horsemen rather than scholars, a certain informality prevails in these bibliographical entries. All references are listed under the name of the author, if possible. Anonymous works and works published under the name of the editor are generally listed by title. Only basic publication information is given here, although the footnotes to the text occasionally contain additional facts about the sources.

Adams, Ott. "Breeding Quarter Horses," *Texas Livestock Journal*, May, 1949.

———. "Credit Given to Shelys," *Western Livestock*, August, 1945.

Albert, Paul. "Romance of the Western Stock Horse," *The Western Horseman*, April, 1936.

The American Farmer. Newspaper ed. by John Stuart Skinner. 11 vols. Baltimore, 1819–29.

The American Stud Book. Vol. VII *et seq*. The Jockey Club, New York, 1898–.

American Turf Register and Sporting Magazine. Vols. I-VI ed. by John Stuart Skinner; Vol. VII ed. by Allen J. Davie; Vols. VIII-IX ed. by Gideon B. Smith; Vols. X-XV ed. by Wm. T. Porter. Baltimore and New York, 1829–44.

Anson, William. "About the Quarter Horse," *The Breeders' Gazette*, August, 1922.

———. *Breeding a Rough Country Horse*. Chicago, 1910. Pamphlet printed for Anson by *The Breeders' Gazette*.

Bateman, Ed. "The Story of My Texas Dandy," *The Quarter Horse*, October, 1948.

———. "The Story of Rialto," *The Quarter Horse*, January, 1948.

Blake, Samuel Coke. "If He Is a Good Horse," *The Ranchman*, April, 1943.

———. "Steel Dust," *The Ranchman*, November, 1948.

———. *The Pride of Mayes County*. Oklahoma, n.d. Pamphlet printed for Blake by The Republican Printery, Pryor.

Browning, Ernest. "He Likes the Using Kind," *The Quarter Horse Journal*, September, 1959.

Bruce, Sanders De Weese. *The American Stud Book*. 6 vols. New York, 1868–94.

———. *Bruce's Turf Register*. Yearly Racing *Report*. Bruce and Company, New York, 1870–75.

Burlingame, Milo. "The Truth About Peter McCue," *Texas Livestock Journal*, December, 1949.

Burns, John. "Breeding Quarter Horses," *The Cattleman*, September, 1942.

Casement, Dan D. "From Punce to Deuce," *The American Hereford Journal*, July, 1954.

———. "The Quarter Horse," *American Cattle Producer*, February, 1941.

———. "Social Significance of the Quarter Horse," *The Cattleman*, September, 1940.

———. "Steel Dusts as I Have Known Them," *The American Hereford Journal*, June, 1927.

Casement, Jack. "Why a Steel Dust Stud Book," *The Western Horseman*, March–April, 1939.

———. "Why We Stick to Steel Dusts," *Western Livestock Journal*, October, 1940.

Cottom, Peter, ed. *Mason's Farrier and Stud-Book—New Edition. The Gentleman's New Pocket Farrier*. 6th ed. Richmond, 1833.

Cullum, Major Grove. "The Quarter Horse," *Horse and Horseman*, May, 1939.

———. "The Western Horse," *Polo*, January, 1935.

Denhardt, Robert Moorman. *The Horse of the Americas*. Norman, 1947.

————. "New Light on Old Steeldust," *The Western Horseman*, November–December, 1939.

————. "Peter McCue, A Wonder Horse," *The Cattleman*, October, 1939.

————. *The Quarter Horse*. 3 vols. Amarillo, 1941–50.

————. "The Quarter Horse, Then and Now," *The Western Horseman*, January, 1939.

————, and Helen Michaelis. *The Quarter Horse, Why He Is What He Is*. Eagle Pass. 1945. Pamphlet printed for the American Quarter Horse Association.

Denhardt Files. These files consist of letters, interviews, pictures, tear sheets, notes, pamphlets, and other records accumulated by Robert Denhardt and the late Helen Michaelis. They are located in Denhardt's home in Arbuckle, California.

Dinsmore, Wayne. "The Racing Record of Peter McCue," *The Quarter Horse Journal*, February, 1964.

Dobie, J. Frank. "Billy Horses and Steel Dusts," *The Cattleman*, March, 1937.

Edgar, Patrick Nisbett. *The American Race-Turf Register, Sportsman's Herald and General Stud Book*. New York, 1833.

Eggleston, Edward. "Husbandry in Colonial Times," *Century Magazine*, January, 1884.

Estes, J. A. "Folklore of the South West," *The Blood Horse*, January, 1944.

Flieger, Joe. "Shue Fly, the Greatest Quarter Horse," *The Western Horseman*, June, 1944.

Flint, Don. "Coke T. Roberds," *The Western Horseman*, November, 1946.

Gard, Wayne. *Fabulous Quarter Horse Steel Dust*. New York, 1958.

————. "Hoofbeats of Old Shiloh," *The Cattleman*, September, 1953.

————. "New Light on Old Shiloh," *The Quarter Horse Journal*, December, 1955.

———. *Sam Bass*. New York, 1936.

———. "When Texas Shouted For Shiloh," *The Western Horseman*, August, 1949.

Gordan, Adam. "Journal of an Officer Who Traveled in America and the West Indies in 1764 and 1765," *Travels in the American Colonies*. New York, 1916.

Graham, Robert Bontine Cunninghame. *The Horses of the Conquest*. London, 1930.

The Half-Breed Stud Book. 2 vols. New York, 1925 and 1930. Printed for the Genesee Valley Breeders' Association.

Hall, J. Goodman. "The Quarter Horse and Quarter Racing," *The Cattleman*, September, 1941.

Harrison, Fairfax. *The Background of the American Stud Book*. Richmond, 1933.

———. *The Equine F. F. V's*. Richmond, 1928.

Haskell, Melville H. *Racing Quarter Horses*. 2 pamphlets. Tucson, 1943 and 1944. Printed for The Southern Arizona Horse Breeders Association.

———. *The Quarter Running Horse*, 5 pamphlets. Tucson, 1945–50. Printed for The American Quarter Racing Association.

Hellbusch, Cecil. "Coke T. Roberds," *The Quarter Horse Journal*, July, 1958.

Hendrix, John. "Pan Zareta," *The Cattleman*, September, 1945.

Herbert, Henry William. *Frank Forester's Horse and Horsemanship of the United States*. 2 vols. New York, 1857.

Hildreth, Samuel C. *The Spell of the Turf*. Philadelphia, 1926.

Holt, Harry. "Famous for Quarter Horses," *The Abilene Reporter News*, August 25, 1942.

Huffington, J. M. "Dan Tucker in Illinois," *The Quarter Horse*, July, 1949.

———. "The Story of Peter McCue," *The Quarter Horse*, September, 1948.

Hunter, Bob. "George Clegg, Veteran Breeder of Top Quarter Horses," *Western Livestock Journal*, May, 1941.

Kelton, Elmer. "Early Quarter Horse Home to be Stocked," *The Quarter Horse Journal*, February, 1963.

Kleberg, Robert J., Jr., and A. O. Rhoad, "The Development of a Superior Family in the Modern Quarter Horse," *The Journal of Heredity*, August, 1946.

Lea, Tom. *The King Ranch*. 2 vols. Boston, 1957.

Mason, Richard. *Mason's Farrier and Stud-Book—New Edition. The Gentleman's New Pocket Farrier*. See Peter Cottom and John Stuart Skinner.

Michaelis, Helen Hall. "The Billy Horse," *Western Livestock Journal*, May, 1941.

————. "Copper Bottom," *Western Livestock Journal*, October, 1941.

————. "Dan Tucker," *Western Livestock Journal*, May, 1942.

————. "Earliest American Horse Breed," *The Cattleman*, September, 1942.

————." King, South Texas Quarter Horse." *The Cattleman*, September, 1944.

————. "The Racing Career of Bob Wade," *Western Livestock Journal*, February, 1942.

National Quarter Horse Breeders' Association Permanent Stud Book. Ed. by J. M. Huffington. 2 vols. Houston, 1947–48.

Nordyke, Lewis. "Traveler Country," *The Quarter Horse Journal*, December, 1954.

Northway, Dr. J. K. "Like Begets Like," *The Cattleman*, September, 1965.

Nye, Nelson C. *Champions of the Quarter Track*. New York, 1950.

————. *The Complete Book of the Quarter Horse*. New York, 1964.

————. *Outstanding Modern Quarter Horse Sires*. New York, 1948.

————. "The Story of Midnight," *The Quarter Horse*, March, 1948.

O'Conner, John L. "The Quarter Horse in Early Days," *The Blood Horse*, October, 1942.

Official Stud Book and Registry of the American Quarter Horse Association. Vol. 1, No. 1–. Fort Worth, Eagle Pass, and Amarillo, 1941–.

The Quarter Horse Breeder. Ed. by M. H. Lindeman. Wichita Falls, 1959.

The Quarter Horse News. (Edited first by Hyde Merritt then by Chuck King.) Colorado Springs, 1950–51. Newspaper printed by *The Western Horseman,* appearing biweekly, with Vol. I, No. 1, appearing on July 7, 1950, and the last issue, Vol. I, No. 14, ending publication on January 25, 1951. Basically it furnished show results but also carried rodeo news, a stallion directory, and feature articles.

The Quarter Running Horse. See under Melville Haskell.

Reynolds, Franklin. "His Blood is Everywhere," *Western Livestock,* May, 1949.

————. "Yellow Jacket, a Most Wonderful Horse," *The Quarter Horse Journal,* June, 1959.

Ridgeway, William. *Origin and Influence of the Thoroughbred Horse.* Cambridge, 1905.

Rules and Regulations of Quarter Racing. Tucson, 1950. Pamphlet printed for the American Quarter Horse Association, Racing Division.

Semotan, Evelyn P. "Old Fred, A Famous Stud," *The Quarter Horse Journal,* December, 1955.

Skinner, John Stuart, ed. *Mason's Farrier and Stud-Book—New Edition. The Gentleman's New Pocket Farrier.* 8th ed. Philadelphia, 1854.

Smelker, Van A., Jr. *The Quarter Running Horse.* Tucson, 1949. Pamphlet printed for the American Quarter Horse Association, Racing Division.

Smiley, H. D. "The Cherokee Side of the Quarter Horse," *The Quarter Horse Journal,* December, 1954.

Smillie, A. F., "Jack." "Red Dog, A Most Surprising Horse," *The Western Horseman,* November, 1965.

Smyth, J. F. D. *A Tour in the United States of America Contain-*

ing an Account of the Present Situation of that Country. 2 vols. London, 1784.

Stinson, W. Claud. "The Story of Chief," Ed. by Ed Bateman. *The Quarter Horse,* February, 1947.

Thoroughbred Racing and Breeding. Ed. by Tom R. Underwood. Baltimore, 1945.

Torey, Sol. "Quarter Horse and Chickasaw," *The Western Horseman,* July, 1942.

Wall, John F. *A Horseman's Handbook on Practical Breeding.* Washington, 1942.

Wallace, John H. *The Horse of America.* New York, 1897.

―――. *Wallace's American Stud-Book, Being a Compilation of the Pedigrees of American and Imported Horses.* New York, 1867.

Welsh, William. "Peter McCue's Family Tree," *The Quarter Horse Journal,* February, 1949.

Wilkinson, Garford. "George Clegg. Pioneer Breeder of Top Quarter Horses," *The Quarter Horse Journal,* January, 1959.

―――. "Jess Hankins, 13th President of the AQHA," *The Quarter Horse Journal,* April, 1964.

―――. "M. Benevides Volpe," *The Quarter Horse Journal,* August, 1962.

Youatt, William. *The Horse.* London, 1883.

"Zantanon," *The Ranchman,* May, 1947.

INDEX

183

11-point Linotype Times Roman is the type face selected for *Quarter Horses*. Originally designed for a London newspaper by Stanley Morison, Times Roman is a highly legible and satisfactory type for almost every reading purpose.